CAVES *of the* APE-MEN

SOUTH AFRICA'S CRADLE OF HUMANKIND WORLD HERITAGE SITE

Ronald J. Clarke • Timothy C. Partridge
With contributions by Kathleen Kuman

An artist's impression of *Australopithecus africanus*.

Cradle of Humankind©
● World Heritage Site

First published in South Africa by:

S.E. Publications (PTY) Ltd
PO Box 75679
Pretoria 0040
South Africa

Distribution by:

Wits University Press
1 Jan Smuts Avenue
Johannesburg
http:/witspress.wits.ac.za
South Africa

First Published 2010

ISBN 978-1-86814-510-2

Publisher/Managing Editor: Susie Jordan Partridge

Authors: Ronald J. Clarke and Timothy C. Partridge

Design, layout and selected illustrations by Flow Communications (PTY) Ltd
PO Box 2222   7 Douglas Street
Highlands North   Waverley
2037   Johannesburg
Johannesburg   South Africa
South Africa
www.flowsa.com

Printed and bound by Paarl Printing (PTY) Ltd
PO Box 248
Paarl
7620
South Africa

Inside the Sterkfontein Caves, the Cradle of Humankind's most famous fossil site.

Contents

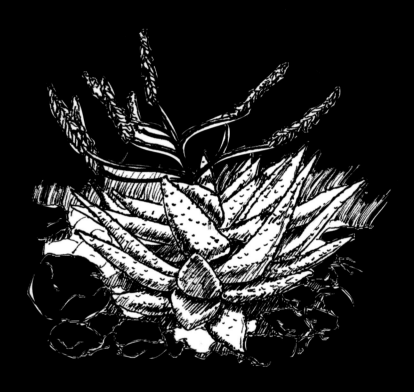

Red hot poker, found in The Cradle of Humankind.

TRIBUTE
Tim Partridge

It is with deep sadness that we record here the sudden death of Tim Partridge on December 8th 2009 whilst he was finalising the production of this book, which will now serve as a memorial to his lifetime of work on the stratigraphy and dating of the caves of the ape-men. Tim will be greatly missed by his many friends and colleagues around the world. He was a leading figure in the fields of geology and palaeoclimatology, and a lover of life, art and science. His generous spirit lives on, and we dedicate this book to his memory.
Ron Clarke and Kathleen Kuman

Professor Tim Partridge was the first to provide firm estimates of the dates of such famous caves as Taung, Sterkfontein, Makapansgat and Swartkrans. This lifelong endeavour, and the breakthroughs that Partridge achieved, made a fundamental contribution to the placement of the early hominids in time. Thus, he enabled us to link them to their ancient chums from East Africa. He revealed the circumstances of life, the environment and ecology, against which the development of humankind took place. It is not surprising that he served as a consultant to our Palaeo-anthropology Research Unit for nearly forty years.
Phillip Tobias

To my beloved husband, Professor Timothy Cooper Partridge, your patience, understanding and support along with hours of hard work, day and night, to make this book a 'first' of its kind out of Africa, pays tribute to your great knowledge and success in life, as it is no doubt in death. Even though our happiness was tragically cut short after just ten weeks of a marriage made in heaven, working with you and your great determination to finish this book for me especially, will keep your memory in my heart and soul forever. I love you.
Susie Jordan Partridge

Tim Partridge with colleagues Alun Hughes, Ian Watt and Justin Wilkinson at Sterkfontein in the 1980s.

View of a cave opening looking up from inside the Sterkfontein Caves.

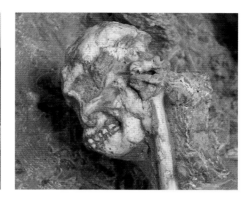

FOREWORD

The publication of this book coincided with the tenth anniversary of the Cradle of Humankind World Heritage Site, which was inscribed by UNESCO on 2 December 1999. The language of *Caves of the Ape-Men* is deliberate, clear and accessible to an audience of non-specialist readers. Professor Ron Clarke, an internationally renowned palaeoanthropologist, teamed up with Professor Tim Partridge, a world authority on chronological analysis of caves, to produce this inspirational book.

The production of this book bears testimony to the continued co-operation between the Gauteng Provincial Government, particularly the Cradle of Humankind World Heritage Site Management Authority, the authors of this book and other academics of the University of the Witwatersrand.

Sterkfontein Caves is not only the single richest hominid fossil site in the world, but it is also home to the longest continuous palaeoanthropological dig. Charles Darwin correctly predicted that science would one day demonstrate how human ancestors originated in Africa. This book examines how a major portion of the South African contribution in support of this bold claim has been located, extracted, analysed and interpreted. The authors relate the history of the search for the human ancestors, animal fossils and stone tools which have contributed to the growing body of evidence for evolution. *Caves of the Ape-Men* reveals the huge amount of information which has been assembled on the origins and proliferation of the bipedal primates called hominids, which includes direct human ancestors, as well as a broad variety of other human-like species which are now extinct. Ron Clarke and Tim Partridge must be commended for the production of this truly professional, accessible and highly attractive book. It is meticulously researched and written, carefully edited, and spectacularly illustrated.

The significance of the African origins of humankind cannot be overemphasised. Africa has produced incontestable evidence of the evolution of the first humans, the first human cultures, the first human use of fire and the ancestors of every single person living on the earth's surface today, no matter how much they may vary in physical attributes, language or culture. All people of South Africa, Africa and the world need to understand the deep significance of the Cradle of Humankind World Heritage Site.

We believe that *Caves of the Ape-Men* will prove indispensible to every person who claims to have a real interest in this fascinating and complex subject.

It is a great loss to the scientific community that Professor Partridge died unexpectedly during the final stages of the production of this book. May *Caves of the Ape-Men* stand as a tribute to his superb scholarship and deep understanding of the complexities and antiquity of human origins.

The Cradle of Humankind World Heritage Site Management Authority

Aerial view of the Cradle of Humankind.

INTRODUCTION

There is a place, not far from Johannesburg in South Africa, where, entombed in the calcified deposits of ancient caves, are fossil bones of our ancestors and the extinct animals which populated that region. This place is now known as the Cradle of Humankind World Heritage Site.

Interior views of the Sterkfontein Caves.

To many people the answer to the question 'where do we come from?' is simple. They consider that humans were specially created. Throughout the world different peoples have creation stories which explain the origin of the highly intelligent animal that has called itself man. It is, in fact, this very intelligence that leads us to wonder about our origins. No other living form does that, because none investigates and analyses itself and its environment in the way that humans do.

A major problem with creation stories arises when one considers the anatomy of humans and realises that we were not specially created because we have characteristics that are found in other animals, and also because we possess some features that make no sense whatsoever, except in terms of their development out of another or earlier form. For example, humans have a coccyx or the remnant of a tail. They also have a premaxillary bone in the front of the palate, and they have a useless appendix.

If we developed out of some earlier form of animal, then it would clearly have been similar to the modern animals closest to us both in anatomy and behaviour, which are the apes. Thus in the 19th Century some interested researchers began to look for fossil remains of the supposed link between ape and man. Because such a transitional form had not yet been found, it became popularly known as the 'missing link.' The first such link, found in Europe, was Neanderthal man. However, apart from having ape-like, large, projecting brow ridges, Neanderthals were essentially human in form and behaviour and so were called *Homo neanderthalensis* – merely a different species of human being. The next major discovery was by the Dutch physician, Eugene Dubois, who in 1891 discovered on the banks of the Solo River at Trinil in Java, Indonesia, a skull cap of a primitive form of human. It was low-browed, with thick projecting brow ridges, but with a much smaller brain than that of modern humans and Neanderthals. Dubois named it *Pithecanthropus erectus* – the erect walking ape-man.

It was to be in South Africa in 1924 that the first of the more ape-like missing links would be found, at the Buxton Limeworks near Taung. The fossilised skull of a child that had human-like teeth but ape-like face and ape-sized brain led Raymond Dart to suggest that it was an evolutionary link between ape and man; he named it *Australopithecus africanus* (the southern ape of Africa). His claims were dismissed by many of his colleagues, but one man, Robert Broom, supported him and was destined to uncover additional intermediate links in the area of the Sterkfontein Caves, the place that is now known as the Cradle of Humankind World Heritage Site. Here Broom discovered in the ancient cave infillings, not only adult *Australopithecus* fossils, but also a second kind of ape-man that he called *Paranthropus* and the fossil remains of very early members of our own genus, *Homo*.

Broom had become the doyen of South African palaeontologists through his early studies, while conducting a country medical practice, of the 250-million-year-old fossils of the Karoo. He had shown these extinct fossil reptiles to have features which placed them early on the evolutionary path leading to the warm-blooded, fur-covered mammals which came to populate the earth during the past 50 million years. As early as 1925 Broom had accepted the Taung Child as a human ancestor, distinct from members of the ape family such as orang utans, chimpanzees and gorillas.

Like Dart, Broom believed, however, that the Taung Child had features intermediate between apes and man, justifying the popular name 'ape-man'. Broom's support for Dart was given in the face of ongoing international opposition to this claim: to some critics the Taung Skull was none other than a juvenile chimpanzee! The young age of the Taung Child at its time of death – no more than four years – was at the heart of this debate. In the apes, some of the features that form the characteristic shape of the skull do not reach their full development until much further along the path between birth and adulthood.

Dart busied himself with other matters as the debate raged on, but some of his students, who were certainly aware of the issues at stake, were inspired to collect and study fossils. In 1935 and 1936 three of them (T. Jones, H. le Riche and G.W.H. Schepers) visited the caves at Sterkfontein where quarrying for stalagmite to produce lime was in progress on the surface hillside above the underground caverns. The lime quarry had encountered a reddish brown, heavily cemented, stony deposit (breccia) which contained the fossilised bones of animals. This deposit was very different from the surrounding bluish grey, layered dolomite bedrock which forms the hilly country of the Cradle. Layers of pure white stalagmite occurred within the breccia and also separated it from the surrounding dolomite bedrock. It was these layers that had attracted the quarrymen, as they could be extracted, crushed and burnt in kilns to form slaked lime, which was in wide demand in the gold mining and building industries.

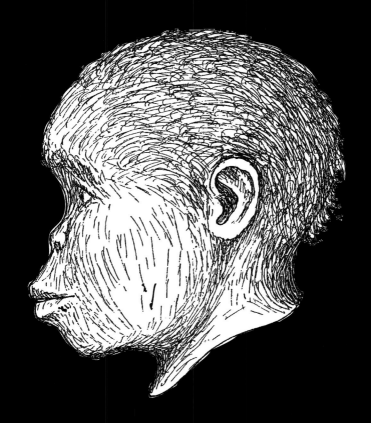

Broom's drawing of the Taung Child.

Above left: G. Martinaglia who first laid bare the fossil-bearing breccias at Sterkfontein, photographed here with his wife.
Above right: Lime kiln at Sterkfontein.

The stalagmite deposits at Sterkfontein had, in fact, been known since 1896, when they were first uncovered by G. Martinaglia, lessee of the local mineral rights. There can be no doubt that the decades of quarrying at Sterkfontein that took place during the first part of the 20th Century played a decisive role in revealing the extent of the bone-bearing deposits there; what remained unknown until the visits of Dart's students in 1935 and 1936 was to what creatures the bones belonged.

Since Dart himself was pursuing other interests, Le Riche and Schepers took their fossils to Robert Broom at the Transvaal Museum. Broom was sufficiently interested to accompany the students back to Sterkfontein on 9th August 1936 and to alert the quarry manager to the kind of bone remains he was seeking. Almost miraculously, a natural cast in breccia of the inside of the braincase of the first specimen of an adult ape-man was presented to Broom on his third visit eight days later, and he also found in the quarry parts of the cranium into which it fitted. This slightly built, small-brained creature had been named *Australopithecus africanus* by Dart on the basis of his earlier study of the Taung Skull. As a group, its representatives are called australopithecines. Probably the most famous of the early specimens of this group is the skull known as Mrs Ples, blasted out of the quarry at Sterkfontein in 1947. More recently, the discovery of an almost complete australopithecine skeleton by Ron Clarke, Stephen Motsumi and Nkwane Molefe in 1997, has attracted renewed interest in Sterkfontein, both from scientists and the public.

This outstandingly important find revealed, for the first time, those special features of the hands and feet that enabled these early South African ape-men to move effectively both on the ground and in the forest canopy.

The trail-blazing finds at Sterkfontein in the years preceding the Second World War, were the first of many in the area. In 1938 the remains of a different, more robust, ape-man were found at Kromdraai, about 1.6 km east of Sterkfontein. This form was named *Paranthropus robustus* by Broom (*Paranthropus* for short). The war years interrupted most scientific work in the area, but in 1948 a mandible and teeth of *Paranthropus*, similar to those from Kromdraai, were found by Broom and his assistant John Robinson at Swartkrans, about 1.2 km west of Sterkfontein. This was followed by the discovery of many more specimens of the same creature, and Swartkrans soon became the richest ape-man site yet discovered. Remarkable, too, was the recovery there, in 1949, of a more advanced (i.e. more human-like) specimen, represented by a lower jaw and a portion of a skull. Now formally placed within the human family (the genus *Homo*), this creature was eventually assigned to the species *Homo ergaster*. Its discovery showed for the first time that three different hominids had lived in the same relatively small area during the time when the fossils accumulated. Further finds at these sites, and the discovery of several new sites in subsequent years, confirmed the presence of at least two different ape-men and one representative of the early human lineage within the Cradle. An outline of the history of these discoveries is given in Chapter 1. Their importance was enormous as, by the early 1950s the sheer weight of information provided by the dozens of ape-man specimens then available for international study had convinced the world of science of the validity of Dart's claims of 25 years earlier.

The times when these different hominids occupied the area were not yet clear, as there was then no reliable way to judge the age of these fossils. The question of age was, in fact, resolved (and then not very accurately) after 1959, when techniques based on the decay of small quantities of radioactive material were first applied to the dating of a newly discovered ape-man site at Olduvai Gorge, Tanzania, and other sites in the Rift Valley of East Africa.

This technique is dependent on the fact that volcanic material (lava, ash and pumice) was erupted regularly from the many active volcanoes lining the floor of the Rift Valley at the time when the ape-man remains were becoming buried by the natural accumulation of lake and river deposits. When these volcanic materials are associated with the burial layer they can be used for accurate dating, since, immediately after eruption, the small radioactive component within them begins to decay into other substances. The extent to which this decay has occurred can be measured in sensitive instruments known as mass spectrometers to give the time that has elapsed since the eruption took place.

No volcanic materials were entrapped within the South African ape-man-bearing deposits because South Africa has had no recent volcanic eruptions, but bones of species of animals which inhabited both East and South Africa at specific times in the past were dated at some of the Rift Valley sites. Because animals can take long periods to migrate from area to area, and because some species which are now extinct survived for long periods in the dated fossil record, correlation of this kind can only provide a rough indication of age. The layers at Sterkfontein containing the australopithecine fossils provide an illustration: only about 40% of the animal species accompanying these remains are present in the dated African fossil record after 2 million years ago, suggesting a substantial age for both. It is only recently that other techniques and better laboratory equipment have been developed which have the potential to provide direct dates for the fossils and deposits in the Cradle of Humankind (see Chapter 2).

What makes the fossil sites of the Cradle unique? To begin with, no such concentration of sites and numbers of fossil specimens documenting our early ancestry have been found anywhere else in the world. As of today, fifteen such sites are on record. Nine of these have produced fossil ape-men (*Australopithecus* and *Paranthropus*), four of these have also yielded remains of *Homo ergaster*, and eight sites have produced Earlier Stone Age tools, probably made by early *Homo*. The tally of fossil hominid specimens recovered from all sites in the area now exceeds eight hundred, making the Cradle by far the richest source in the

Interior views of Sterkfontein Caves showing dolomite pendants which remained when the surrounding dolomite was slowly dissolved by slightly acidic water beneath the water table.

world of information on the origins of our species. Foremost among the sites of the Cradle is Sterkfontein, where more than five hundred specimens of two types of ape-men, one kind of human, two kinds of early stone tools as well as fossil wood have been found; it also boasts a large site museum where key finds are on display.* That this huge body of evidence comes from Africa is a powerful vindication of the prediction of the great naturalist, Charles Darwin, made in his book of 1871, *The Descent of Man*, that Africa would prove to be the cradle of humanity.

The ape-man sites of the Cradle are unique, too, in the manner in which fossils have been trapped and preserved within them. The bedrock of the area is dolomite, a bluish grey rock formed beneath the sea more than 2000 million years ago. This rock is soluble in rainwater percolating down natural fissures within it. As percolation continues through time, the fissures are enlarged into vertical chimneys which lead down to the water table (the level below which all cavities within the rock mass remain filled with water).

At the water table, and just below it, much more widespread solution occurs to form large, water-filled caverns. With time, the water level drops, the caverns fill with air and become coated with calcareous formations (stalactites and stalagmites) as rainwater percolates through the rock from above. Collapse of parts of the unstable roofs of the caverns enlarge the chimneys and create openings to the land surface

* A more ambitious Museum and Visitor Centre were established by the Gauteng Provincial Government in 2005 at Maropeng, about 10 km from Sterkfontein (see Chapter 8).

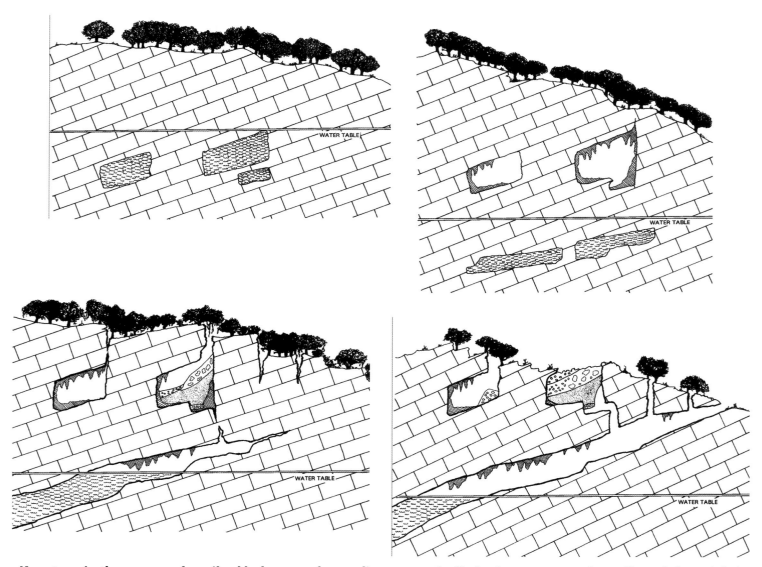

Key steps in the process described below are shown diagrammatically in the sequence above (from left to right).

above. At this point the caves become accessible to surface soil and to the bone remains that accumulated around the openings of the chimneys as a result of death, or of the activities of predatory and scavenging animals. These surface materials collect in piles beneath the chimneys, where they are infiltrated by dripping water which is strongly charged with calcium carbonate from the solution of the dolomite. In due course, the calcium carbonate cements the entire mass into a rock-like breccia. Key steps in the process described above are shown diagrammatically in the figure above.

Almost all of the fossil-bearing deposits of the Cradle have formed in this way. Of importance is the fact that the caverns where the breccia accumulated via vertical shafts would have been inaccessible to ape-men and even to nimble monkeys. In other words, the shafts acted as conduits for bones lying on the surface or as death traps for creatures unfortunate enough to stumble into them. This topic is explored further in Chapter 2 because it is very important in determining what parts of a skeleton are most commonly preserved in the breccia.

SITE NAME	APE-MEN (Australopithecus)	APE-MEN (Paranthropus)	EARLY HOMO (Homo ergaster)	STONE TOOLS	OTHER DISCOVERIES
Sterkfontein	More than 500 specimens	A few specimens	Yes	Yes (Oldowan, Early Acheulean, & Middle Stone Age industries)	Fossil wood, fossil animals, a second (unnamed) species of Australopithecus
Swartkrans	No	More than 200 specimens	Yes	Yes (Probable Oldowan, Early Acheulean, and Middle Stone Age industries)	Burnt bones, fossil animals
Kromdraai B	No	Yes	No	Yes (2 or 3 Oldowan artefacts)	Fossil animals
Kromdraai A	No	No	No	Yes (over 100 Early Acheulean artefacts)	Fossil animals
Cooper's	No	Yes	No	Yes	Fossil animals
Bolt's Farm	No	No	No	No	Fossil animals
Goldsmith's	No	No	No	Yes (10)	Fossil animals
Drimolen	No	More than 80 specimens	Yes	Yes (a few)	Fossil animals
Plover's Lake	No	No	No	Yes (Middle Stone Age)	Fossil animals
Gladysvale	Two teeth	No	No	Yes (one from the younger deposits)	Fossil animals
Motsetsi	No	No	No	No	Fossil animals
Gondolin	No	One tooth	One tooth Homo?	No	Fossil animals
Haasgat	No	No	No	No	Fossil animals
Minnaars	No	No	No	No	Fossil animals
Makapansgat	Yes	No	No	Yes (from the younger deposits)	Fossil animals
Taung	One (Taung Child)	No	No	Yes (no early tools, some later Stone Age tools from some caves)	Fossil animals

Fossil finds from the various fossil sites in the Cradle of Humankind.

The lower-lying deposits at the bottoms of these shafts have recently yielded important specimens, including the almost complete australopithecine skeleton known as Little Foot. Access to the underground caverns at Sterkfontein was provided in the 1930s as an added attraction for visitors who flocked to the site in the wake of the publicity that followed Broom's early discoveries. A few of the cave sites (such as Gladysvale) developed in a different way. Here the caves opened into the sides of valleys and were more easily accessible to animals and ape-men than the vertical shafts.

A number of institutions and corporate bodies have made important contributions to the development of infrastructure within the Cradle and to the funding of research carried out at its various fossil sites. Foremost amongst these is the University of the Witwatersrand, which owns the land on which the Sterkfontein and Swartkrans sites are located, and which has assumed responsibility for the research carried out at those sites. Excavations by its staff have, in fact, continued unbroken at Sterkfontein since 1966 and research at other sites in the Cradle has been conducted more intermittently by other of its scientists. The Transvaal Museum (now the Ditsong National Natural History Museum) has, in the past, been active at Sterkfontein, Swartkrans and Kromdraai, as has been recounted above.

More recently, the Standard Bank of South Africa has played an active role in promoting heritage projects in the Cradle. Not only was it a founding partner in the Palaeoanthropology Scientific Trust (PAST), but it continues to be the principal corporate sponsor of this body. PAST funds a broad spectrum of research within the Cradle, including the ongoing excavation at Sterkfontein; when the latter's continuance was threatened by lack of funds in 1994, it was PAST and the Standard Bank who stepped in to ensure that this work would continue. This investment has led to important new finds, including the Little Foot skeleton.

In September 2001 the Standard Bank donated 100 hectares of a farm which they owned within the Cradle for building the Maropeng Visitor Centre (see Chapter 8). Its programme of annual Standard Bank/PAST Keynote Lectures has brought distinguished international scientists to South Africa to present their findings to the public and to interact with local scientists. Other important contributions by the Standard Bank include educational bursaries for postgraduate students in palaeoanthropology and related fields, not only within South Africa but in countries to the north such as Kenya, Tanzania and Ethiopia.

The chapters which follow are intended to provide a popular, copiously illustrated account of the finds in the Cradle of Humankind and of their importance for the understanding of our own origins. Chapter 1 outlines the historical background to the finds. Chapter 2 provides an overview of the natural environment of the area, and how and when the fossil remains became preserved there in such profusion. Chapter 3 describes the ape-man *Australopithecus*. Chapter 4 portrays a different type of ape-man, the large-toothed, flat-faced *Paranthropus*; Chapter 5 traces the beginning of stone tool-making in the area, the case made for the early use of fire, and the early development of culture; Chapter 6 examines the plants and animals that occurred in the area in the past, while Chapter 7 ventures a glimpse into the future and the risks to humanity posed by disregard for our fragile environment. A final chapter gives further information on the Maropeng Visitor Centre and Sterkfontein Caves.

Chapter ONE
DISCOVERY

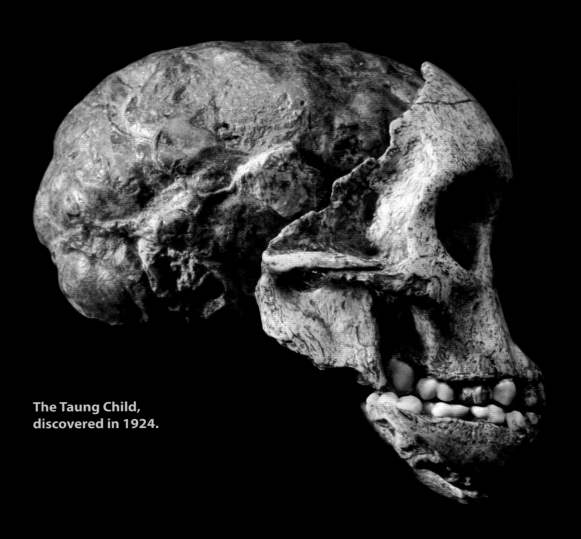

The Taung Child,
discovered in 1924.

18th Century concept of orang utan as depicted by Hulk in Buffon's
Histoire naturelle, générale et particuliére.

Humans belong within the group of animals known as primates, which includes lemurs, lorises, tarsiers, monkeys, apes, as well as ourselves. Humans – and their earlier relatives all within the family of hominidae (hominids) – are unique within this group in having canine teeth of greatly reduced size (when compared to other primates), a habitual two-legged mode of walking, and a long thumb, the tip of which can be opposed against the tips of the other fingers. Humans also possess a large, complex brain. It was this brain, together with the opposable thumb, that permitted the development of advanced culture, which includes the uniquely human pursuits of art and science. Art consists of pictorial, sculptural and other expressions concerning aspects of life and environment. Science is based on questioning – the why, what, where and how of aspects of life and environment and a quest into how things function.

It is this ability of humans to enquire into and analyse their environment that has led to our immense understanding of the form and functioning of the visible universe. We do not know when humans first began to wonder about where they came from and why they were different to animals, but we do know that for most of human history such thoughts have been answered by supernatural explanations – beliefs in gods who created the world and everything in it, and in life after death.

This third uniquely human pursuit (religion) is documented not only in ancient written records but in structures dedicated to the worship of gods and in religious artefacts recovered in archaeological excavations. Human societies were structured around these beliefs; so powerful was religious belief and dogma, and so linked was it to the rulers of society, that to question or contradict any aspect of it was considered anti-social and a heresy punishable by imprisonment or even death. In the early 17th

Above left: Gorilla sitting in a posture where its face seems to be in its chest.
Above right: Orang utan sitting in a similar posture.

Sebastian Munster's illustration of monsters. From left to right, the sciopod that used its one large foot as a sunshade, a one-eyed cyclops, a two-headed midget, a blemmyae with its face in its chest and a dog-headed man, dating to circa 1575, published in *Cosmographen*.

Sebastian Munster's illustration of a wild man and wild woman, dating to circa 1575.

Century the Italian astronomer Galileo was put on trial by the religious inquisition in Rome for proclaiming his finding that the earth revolved around the sun, thus contradicting the belief that the earth was the centre of the universe. He was ordered to retract his claims and was put under house arrest for the last eight years of his life. This religious dogma concerning the universe stifles scientific enquiry and is a denial of what made us human in the first place – our enquiring minds.

In 1758, the Swedish naturalist Linnaeus classified humans within the zoological order Primates, which he defined as containing three genera, *Lemur* (lemurs), *Simia* (monkeys), and *Homo* (orang utan, chimpanzee and humans). Although the chimpanzee and orang utan were classed as human and depicted as standing upright, usually with the aid of a stick, they were thought of as wild men, whilst humans were classified as *Homo sapiens,* meaning wise man.

The gorilla was not to be discovered scientifically until 1855, when Paul du Chaillu first saw a specimen at close quarters. Prior to this the existence of such a creature was hinted at only in traveller tales. Such anecdotes included a variety of monsters, both on land and in the sea, whose existence was based partly on imagination, but also on the misinterpretation of fleeting or distant sightings of real creatures. The blemmyae, a creature with no head but a face in its chest, could well have been conceived from a distant sighting of a male gorilla; these, in a sitting posture, do seem to have their faces in their chests. The hairy wild men (or wodewose) of traveller tales were undoubtedly based on sightings of apes.

Lord Monboddo of Scotland (left) and Charles Darwin (right).

The similarities between apes and humans impressed James Burnet, Lord Monboddo of Scotland (above), to the extent that in 1774, in his book *Origin and Progress of Language*, he wrote, "From the South Sea, I will come back again to Africa, a country of very great extent; in which, if it were well searched, I am persuaded that all the several types of human progression might be traced and perhaps all the varieties of the species discovered." Ten years later, J.W. Goethe of Germany made the first significant discovery linking humans and apes. He found that humans, like apes and other mammals, had a separate segment in their upper jaws (the premaxillary bone) containing the incisor teeth. In the apes this is seen to be separated from the maxilla by sutures (or serrated joins) in the face and a suture in the palate. In humans its presence is detectable only in infants as a suture in the palate dividing the premaxilla from the maxilla (face and upper jaw) which is never visible from the outside. In 1869 G.W. Callender found that, in the human embryo, thin plates of the maxillary bone grow over the facial portion of the premaxilla such that the premaxilla is visible only in the infant palate.

If humans had been a special separate creation, then why would they have retained such a feature? Its continued existence is as a vestigial bone that has become retracted and is covered by the maxillary bones of the face. Logically, it should have been more prominent and more obvious in a fossil ancestor; but where were these fossils? This may sound complicated to those unfamiliar with anatomy, but it is of major importance for an understanding of the reality of the evolutionary process.

The concept of evolution was set out by Charles Darwin in 1859 in his book *On the Origin of Species by Means of Natural Selection*. His principal conclusion was that the diversity of life had come about through new species developing out of earlier species as an adaptation to a particular way of life. Such an explanation was unacceptable to the religious establishment and Darwin was criticised and ridiculed. Such a concept is, however, easier to understand when one sees how a caterpillar changes into a butterfly during its life cycle. Although less easy to observe because of their longer timespan, slight genetic changes over generations can result in a new species developing out of an earlier one.

19th Century photograph of T. H. Huxley.

Fossil bones of mammals, reptiles, fish and shells have been found in many different parts of the world, showing that strange, extinct forms of life have existed in the past. The established explanation for these was that they had all died in the Biblical flood. However, geologists could demonstrate that these creatures did not all die at the same time but came from different geological strata (or layers), often separated by millions of years; there was, in fact, a clear pattern of simple life forms developing over time into more complex forms; these complex forms were never found in the earlier strata together with the simpler forms.

If this was the pattern of development of animal life, could it apply also to the origin of humans? The zoologist T.H. Huxley posed the question in 1863 in his book Man's Place in Nature, when he wrote, "Where then must we look for primeaeval Man? Was the oldest Homo sapiens Pliocene or Miocene, or yet more ancient? In still older strata do the fossilised bones of an ape more anthropoid or a man more pithecoid await the researches of some unborn palaeontologist?"

Two unborn researchers were indeed to fulfil this prophecy. One was Raymond Dart, born in 1893 and destined to be the Professor of Anatomy who would discover the Taung child – the so-called missing link between ape and man. The other was Robert Broom, the Scots doctor born in 1866, who became a palaeontologist renowned for his work on the Karoo mammal-like reptiles (links between reptiles and mammals) and went on to find the first adult missing link at Sterkfontein. In 1866, the same year in which Broom was born, the German zoologist Ernst Haeckel wrote in his *General Morphology*, "It is now an indisputable fact that man is descended from apes." He said further, "I must here also point out, what in fact is self-evident, that not one of all the still living apes, and consequently not one of the so-called man-like apes, can be the progenitor of the human race ... The ape-like progenitors of the

Pithecanthropus alalus was an imagined ancestor of humans, pictured here in an 1894 illustration by Gabriel Max.

human race are long since extinct. We may possibly find their fossil bones in the Tertiary rocks of Southern Asia or Africa." In 1876 in his *History of Creation*, Haeckel proposed a link between ape and man in the form of a speechless ape-man, *Pithecanthropus alalus*, and in 1894 the artist Gabriel Max produced a picture of this imaginary ancestor (above).

At the time of Huxley's book the only known specimens of fossil man were from Europe; some of these were very ancient Homo sapiens and others specimens of Neanderthal man, a massive-browed but large-brained species of human that lived between 130 000 and 28 000 years ago at the same time as Homo sapiens. Huxley wrote that, even though the Neanderthal cranium was the most ape-like known, this and the other skulls did not take us nearer to the lower ape-like form from which humans must have developed.

In 1891 the Dutch physician Eugene Dubois, who had gone to Indonesia specifically to look for a missing link, did indeed find at Trinil, Java, a skullcap – associated with a femur (thigh bone) – that was smaller brained and more primitive, and geologically much older, than Neanderthal man. He named it *Pithecanthropus erectus* – the erect walking ape-man. It is now called *Homo erectus* and is known to have lived over a million years ago. There remained, however, a need for something even more ape-like. In 1856, the year in which the Neanderthal skullcap was found at the Feldhofer cave near Dusseldorf in Germany, a fossilised ape jaw and arm bone were discovered in Miocene (11 to 12 million year old) deposits at Saint Gaudens in France by Edouard Lartet. He named the creature to which these belonged *Dryopithecus fontani*. Thus, as apes and primitive man had existed in Europe, it seemed likely that the missing link should be found there too. This set the stage for the discovery at Piltdown in Sussex, England, between 1912 and 1915, of part of a large, thick human braincase associated with an ape-like mandible. This supposed missing link was widely accepted until 1953, when it was shown to be a forgery consisting of a human braincase and an orang utan jaw, the teeth of which had been filed down to make them look human, and the bone of which had been stained to make it appear fossilised.

Illustration of Piltdown Man by A. Forestier.

Raymond Dart, 1925.

**The quarry face at Buxton Limeworks
showing the breccia-filled cavity at its
centre, from where the Taung Skull was said
to have been blasted out.**

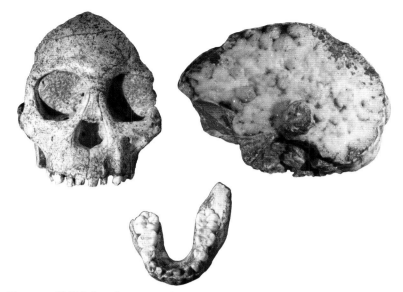

Face of the Taung Child, brain cast (showing calcareous crystals), and the lower jaw.

Meanwhile, the real missing links with small brains and man-like jaws were being found by Dart and Broom in South Africa; these discoveries were, however, dismissed by many researchers as the remains of apes because the Piltdown Man supposedly showed that the missing link should have a large brain and ape-like jaw. In 1924 an ancient cave infilling, that would later prove to contain the skull of a four year-old-ape-man child, was blasted out of a lime quarry at Buxton near Taung, in what is today the North West Province of South Africa. In November 1924 some blocks containing fossil bones had been collected after this blast by a quarry worker, M. de Bruyn, and taken to the office of the quarry manager, A.E. Spiers.

The young Raymond Dart, recently appointed as Professor of Anatomy at the University of the Witwatersrand Medical School in Johannesburg, requested his geologist colleague R.B. Young to send him any fossils he might find while he was visiting the Taung area to inspect the limestone deposits. Young duly arranged for Spiers to send to Dart two boxes of rocks containing fossil bones. In the first Dart found nothing to excite his interest, but in the second box he saw the natural cast, preserved in rock-like calcified cave sediment, of the inside of the braincase of a large primate. This was a natural brain cast which indicated that the creature to which it belonged had a brain larger than that of baboons and other monkeys, but similar in size to that of apes. Dart found that this cast fitted perfectly against another block that showed some traces of bone; when he cleaned away the rock he exposed the magnificent face of a fossil skull with upper and lower jaws with teeth of a child. Although it was superficially chimpanzee-like, it had a smooth brow instead of the prominent brow ridge of a chimp of that young age. Furthermore, the cheek teeth were not those of an ape but were human-like, though very large; the canine tooth was not long, as in a chimp, but short like that of humans. Dart also noted that the position of the opening to the spinal column under the skull indicated that this creature walked upright. Here, then, was the long awaited missing link between ape and man. Dart named it *Australopithecus africanus* – the southern ape of Africa.

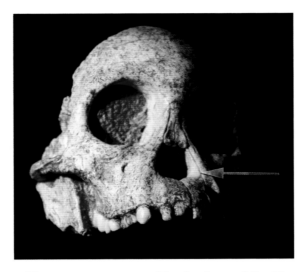

Premaxillary suture arrowed in the face of the Taung Child.

We now know that it lived more than 2 million years ago. Interestingly, the suture between the premaxilla and the maxilla is clearly visible on the face, providing another link between ape and human, as was discussed earlier in this chapter.

Although many of Dart's colleagues did not accept his claims, he found an immediate and staunch supporter in Robert Broom, who accepted the Taung Child as a human ancestor and made it his mission to look for an adult fossil ape-man. His opportunity came when, on the 9th of August 1936, two of Dart's students, Harding le Riche and G.W.H. Schepers, took him for the first time to the Sterkfontein Caves, where they had recovered fossil monkey specimens blasted out by lime miners*. Broom asked the quarry manager, Mr Barlow, if he had ever found anything like the Taung Child; on Broom's third visit on the 17th of August 1936, Barlow handed him a brain cast similar to that from Taung. Broom searched in the rubble from the blasting and found parts of the skull, including teeth, and saw the top of the skull embedded in cave infill in the wall of the quarry.

The skull, catalogued as TM 1511, was badly crushed, but subsequent work at the site has uncovered several more partial skulls, including the famous Mrs Ples found in 1947. At the time when he found the first adult skull Broom was 70 years old but he continued to make major discoveries in the years following until his death in 1951.

In 1938, at the site of Kromdraai just over a kilometre from Sterkfontein, a school boy, Gert Terblanche, showed Broom where he had found parts of a large-toothed, flat-faced skull that Broom classified as a new kind of ape-man, *Paranthropus robustus*. This ape-man lived at Kromdraai about 1.9 million years ago. In 1948 Broom and his young assistant, the zoologist John Robinson, found at Swartkrans near Sterkfontein more fossils of *Paranthropus*. This was followed in 1949 by Robinson's discovery at Swartkrans of a small-toothed mandible of what was called 'true man' to distinguish it from an ape-man. Here was proof of an ancestral human living at the same time as the big-toothed ape-man; it was then named *Telanthropus capensis*, but is now classed as an early form of *Homo*, generally considered to be *Homo ergaster*. This kind of *Homo* would later be found at Sterkfontein in a younger part of the deposit than that which produced the *Australopithecus* fossils. In 1956 and 1957 the same deposit at Sterkfontein yielded to C. K. (Bob) Brain, John Robinson and Revil Mason stone tools of the early Acheulean period.

Robert Broom points to the breccia where he recovered the first adult *Australopithecus*, TM 1511. Next to him is G.W. Barlow, the Sterkfontein quarry manager.

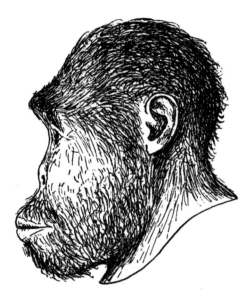

Broom's concept of the appearance of the Kromdraai ape-man, *Paranthropus*.

* *The discovery of the fossil-bearing cave deposits of the Cradle of Humankind was inextricably linked to the early years of gold mining in the Johannesburg area. It was, in fact, some years before the discovery of the extensive gold-bearing reefs of the Witwatersrand in 1885 that traces of the metal were found within the Cradle. In 1881 a gold nugget was recovered on the farm Kromdraai by J.H. Minnaar (after whom the fossil site immediately across the Bloubank River from Sterkfontein is named). The Kromdraai Gold Mining Company extracted gold from rocks of the Black Reef Formation, which adjoins the cavernous dolomite of the Cradle, from 1887 to 1912. The remains of these mine workings continue to attract visitors today. It was, however, the clusters of deep gold mines along the Witwatersrand reefs, extending 70 km from Krugersdorp to Springs, that attracted lime miners to the Cradle. These large gold mines used considerable tonnages of lime to extract the gold from the crushed rock; the demand lessened only in the 1930s with the widespread introduction of cyanide in the gold extraction process. As has already been noted in the Foreword, it was the early lime mining activities of G. Martinaglia at Sterkfontein from 1896 onwards that first laid bare the fossil-bearing breccias at that site. Robert Broom's subsequent discoveries of hominid remains both there and at Kromdraai and Swartkrans would not have been possible without exposure of the fossil deposits by ongoing lime mining at those sites.*

At much the same time another very important fossil cave site was being explored in the northern part of South Africa at Makapansgat, in what is now the Limpopo Province of South Africa. In 1945 Phillip Tobias, a student of Dart, led an expedition to the caves and, on finding fossils, inspired Dart, who had left the field of palaeoanthropology 15 years earlier, to open a search there for more fossil hominids. In 1947 the back portion of a hominid skull was recovered from lime miners' dumps by James Kitching. Dart named the species Australopithecus prometheus.

In 1948 Alun Hughes and Scheepers Kitching recovered from the dumps at Makapansgat a magnificent jawbone of a child with very large teeth. Continued methodical processing of the blocks of ancient cave infill (breccia) in the dumps resulted in the recovery of not only many more *Australopithecus* fossils but also thousands of well preserved fossils of a variety of animals. This massive accumulation of bones was thought by Dart to be the work of *Australopithecus* who, he believed, had used the bones as tools. He invented the name 'Osteodontokeratic culture', meaning bone, tooth and horn culture, and categorised the fossils as a variety of weapons and tools, such as clubs, daggers and saws. It is now known that the bones, including the *Australopithecus* fossils, were accumulated by hyaenas and porcupines.

Dart's numerous publications and lectures providing dramatic portrayals of *Australopithecus* as a bloodthirsty cannibal, wielding clubs like Hercules and jawbones like Samson, certainly popularised the subject of human origins. Furthermore, it inspired research into how bones are accumulated in caves and other deposits. This is the science of taphonomy – or what happens to a body between death and burial. One of the first people to involve himself in such studies was Dart's technical assistant and Makapansgat excavator Alun Hughes, who was convinced that porcupines were largely responsible for the Makapansgat fossil accumulation.

Variants of all three types of hominid from South Africa, *Australopithecus*, *Paranthropus* and early *Homo*, were found subsequently in East Africa in Tanzania, Kenya and Ethiopia. In 1959, Mary and Louis Leakey uncovered at Olduvai Gorge in Tanzania the 1.75 million-year-old skull of a very large toothed *Paranthropus* that they called *Zinjanthropus boisei* (now *Paranthropus boisei*). This was followed by the recovery of skull fragments and the lower jaw of a child that was named in 1964 as a new species, *Homo habilis*, by Louis Leakey, Phillip Tobias and John Napier. *Homo habilis* lived about 1.8 million years ago and was considered to be the maker of the primitive stone tools – choppers, cores and flakes – of the Oldowan industry. In the same year a magnificent *Paranthropus* mandible was spotted by Kamoya Kimeu, projecting from high up in a cliff of ancient lake deposits at Peninj on Lake Natron, during an expedition led by Glynn Isaac and Richard Leakey. These discoveries provided the impetus for exploration by research teams in remote areas of Ethiopia and Kenya. They resulted in the recovery of large numbers of early hominid fossils from volcanic regions which have permitted dating of the fossil deposits by radiometric methods. This intense exploration for early hominid sites yielded remarkable results. Among the discoveries made were remains of the oldest claimed hominid, the 7 million-year-old *Sahelanthropus tchadensis* from Chad, followed in time by the 6 million-year-old *Orrorin tugenensis* from Kenya, the 4.4 million-year-old *Ardipithecus ramidus* from Ethiopia, and the 4.2 million-year-old *Australopithecus anamensis* from Kenya.

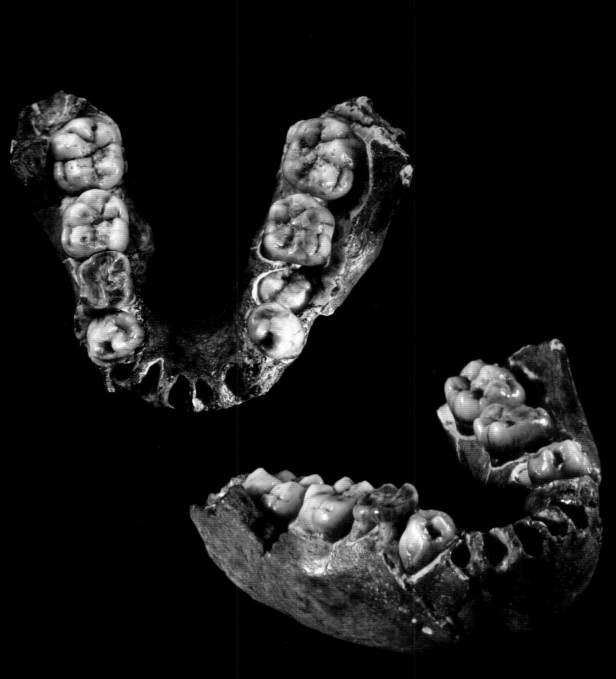

Two views of a child mandible (MLD 2) of the second species of *Australopithecus*, which Dart named *Australopithecus prometheus*, from Makapansgat.

Footprint trail of *Australopithecus afarensis* at Laetoli, Tanzania (3.6 million years old).

Also noteworthy is the 3.6 million year old hominid footprint trail uncovered at Laetoli, Tanzania, which has been attributed to Australopithecus afarensis, fossils of which have been found at Laetoli and at Hadar in Ethiopia. There have been suggestions that the Laetoli hominids are more akin to Australopithecus anamensis and should be classed under an earlier name, 'Praeanthropus africanus', that was given to an upper jaw fragment found at Garusi, Laetoli, in 1939. From Kenya came the 3.6 million-year-old Kenyanthropus platyops and from Ethiopia the 2.5 million-year-old Paranthropus aethiopicus and the 2.5 million-year-old Australopithecus garhi.

The geographic and temporal range of this great variety of human ancestral relatives has demonstrated that there was not just one missing link – or indeed a chain of links – between Miocene ape and modern man; there was, instead, a network of early hominid species, only one lineage of which would eventually lead to modern humans. In the Cradle of Humankind the methodical excavation started in 1966 by Phillip Tobias and Alun Hughes still continues at Sterkfontein, as does work at the nearby Swartkrans site, started in 1966 by Bob Brain. This work, as well as excavations at several other sites in the Cradle of Humankind, continues to uncover many clues to the mysteries of our origins by providing specimens in numbers sufficiently large for us to begin to understand the variability which existed in these early hominid populations.

Cast of the skull of *Paranthropus boisei* (0H 5) from Olduvai Gorge, Tanzania (1.75 million years) and the lower jaw (L7-A-125) from Omo, Ethiopia.

Chapter TWO
LAND, LIFE AND TIME

Paranthropus crania (SK 48 left
and SK 46 right), discovered at
Swartkrans.

Above left: Dolomite rock showing typical elephant skin weathering and a chert layer at the base.
Above right: Dolomite rock at Sterkfontein.

Despite its proximity to the urban metropolis of Pretoria, the Witwatersrand and Vereeniging, in which a quarter of South Africa's people now live, many parts of the Cradle remain sparsely populated and some are almost pristine. Its rugged hills and valleys are the product of a long geological history extending back some 2500 million years.

The dolomite rock which lies beneath much of the Cradle (see the diagram on the following page) is the key to the preservation of the rich treasure-house of fossils which continues to divulge to the world new insights into our origins. As was mentioned in the introduction to this book, slightly acidic water beneath the water table dissolved the dolomite over millions of years to form underground caverns. When the water table dropped and the caves eventually opened to the surface, they became receptacles for soil and bones (and occasionally whole animals) falling into them from the land surface above.

The dolomite of the Cradle was formed when carbonates of calcium and magnesium precipitated out of sea water as chemical sediments in the shallow ocean which covered much of north western South Africa at that time. As the water chemistry changed periodically, layers of chert (silicon dioxide) were formed within the dolomite. The chert is important because it is insoluble in slightly acidic groundwater or rainwater and therefore, when present as a thick layer, tends to form a roof over any cave below; periodical collapse of such roofs created vertical openings, often with overhangs, which precluded entry by surface dwelling animals including ape-men, but acted as death traps for the unwary and as conduits for the bones of those that died on the land surface outside the cave. An important feature of areas underlain by dolomite is that, because of their cavernous nature, they serve as stores of underground water; these subterranean reservoirs feed numerous surface springs so that major valleys in the area such as the Bloubank below Sterkfontein carry perennial streams and probably did so in the past.

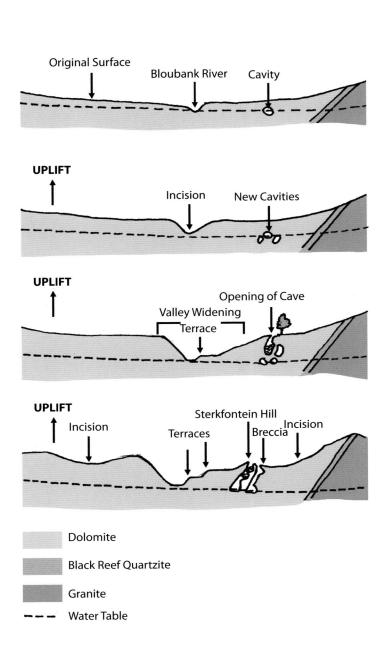

Original Surface　　Bloubank River　　Cavity

UPLIFT

Incision　　New Cavities

UPLIFT

Opening of Cave

Valley Widening

Terrace

UPLIFT

Incision　　Terraces　　Sterkfontein Hill　　Breccia　　Incision

Dolomite

Black Reef Quartzite

Granite

- - - Water Table

Schematic section showing evolution of the Bloubank River valley and the Sterkfontein Cave system.

Cave openings looking from inside the caves and up at a shaft at Sterkfontein.

The Cradle is situated on the elevated interior plateau of South Africa about 1480 metres above sea level. Repeated uplifts of the land surface as a result of processes deep within the earth were responsible for the formation of this high plateau; these movements also caused rivers such as the Bloubank to cut down in their valleys; this, in turn, lowered the level of the water table and caused the water-filled caverns to dry out. As the valleys were deepened they also became widened, resulting in the opening of some of the caverns (see diagram on opposite page).

The floors of the river valleys were covered with alluvial deposits, which included sands and gravels washed down by the rivers. Some of the gravels were transported long distances and include rocks such as quartzite and diabase that do not otherwise occur in close proximity to the fossil sites.

As successive cycles of valley deepening occurred, some of these alluvial deposits were abandoned on the sides of the valleys as river terraces. Their foreign rocks, particularly the quartzite (a hard, altered silicate rock) provided local, easily accessible sources of material which were used by the first tool-making hominids to inhabit the Cradle *(Homo)* to fashion stone tools (or artefacts). Quartzite is a hard rock, good for tool making, but quartz, chert and diabase from the gravels were used also, as well as chert weathering out from hard, siliceous bands within the cave dolomite (see Chapter 5).

Bones collect on the surface, find their way into the caves, and in some cases they can become distributed within the cave system by internal processes. All of these mechanisms provide important clues on the way of life of the early ape-men and the environment in which they lived. The study of these mechanisms has become a sophisticated and specialised field of research known as taphonomy.

Landscape of the Cradle of Humankind.

An extensive range of taphonomic processes can operate in and around caves. For example, the selection and degree of fragmentation of the bones accumulating on the surface above the cave is different when they are as a result of butchering by hominids, as distinct from the hunting activities of carnivorous animals such as lions and hyaenas. Animal food remains dropped by leopards feeding in trees above the cave mouths are also distinctive, as are the complete skeletons that are preserved below cave openings when these acted as death traps (which was probably the case with Little Foot).

The composition of the bone assemblage is changed yet further as fragments are re-distributed down the sides of a debris or talus cone which is formed below an opening or are washed into deep cave recesses. Each set of circumstances serves as a filter which changes the character of the assemblage by selectively removing certain shapes and sizes (e.g., if the transporting power of stormwater flows entering the cave is sufficient to carry away the smaller bone fragments only). The nature of the cave deposits themselves may provide independent clues on the mechanisms at work: large scale layering usually indicates the action of slowly flowing water, while, on a debris cone, well defined layers containing fine sediments are indicative of mud flows. Slowly flowing water is less effective as a transporting agent than are successive mud flows. It is the need to interpret such complex information that requires the input of a team of scientists, each with a particular field of expertise, if the history preserved within the cave deposits is to be properly comprehended and interpreted.

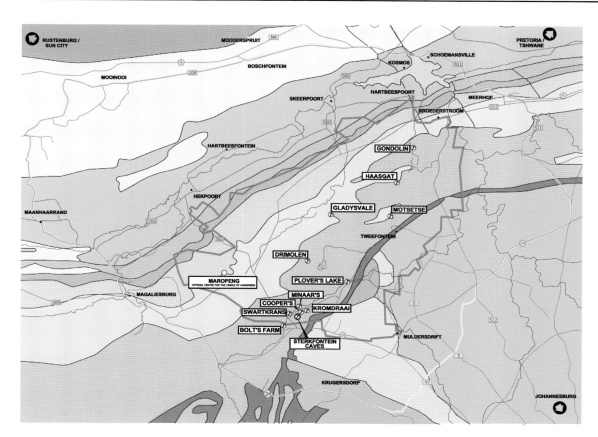

GEOLOGICAL LEGEND

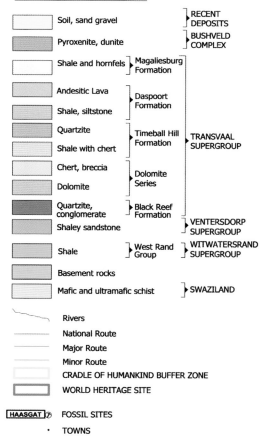

Soil, sand gravel		RECENT DEPOSITS
Pyroxenite, dunite		BUSHVELD COMPLEX
Shale and hornfels	Magaliesburg Formation	
Andesitic Lava	Daspoort Formation	
Shale, siltstone		
Quartzite	Timeball Hill Formation	TRANSVAAL SUPERGROUP
Shale with chert		
Chert, breccia	Dolomite Series	
Dolomite		
Quartzite, conglomerate	Black Reef Formation	
Shaley sandstone		VENTERSDORP SUPERGROUP
Shale	West Rand Group	WITWATERSRAND SUPERGROUP
Basement rocks		
Mafic and ultramafic schist		SWAZILAND

Rivers	
National Route	
Major Route	
Minor Route	
CRADLE OF HUMANKIND BUFFER ZONE	
WORLD HERITAGE SITE	

HAASGAT ⑦ FOSSIL SITES

· TOWNS

Geographical Map of the Cradle of Humankind.

Zebras prefer a grassy, savannah environment.

The cave deposits and their fossil remains can also tell us a great deal about the kind of vegetation which covered the area in the time of the ape-men. Today's vegetation has been disturbed, particularly along the major river valleys such as the Bloubank, where abundant water makes intensive agriculture possible; but on some intervening ridges and in the remoter valleys the vegetation is well-nigh pristine. Over large areas the natural vegetation is a sparse Rhus and Protea savannah (mainly Rhus pyroides, Rhus lancea, Protea caffra and Protea rupelliae, separated by swathes of tussock grass); this occupies the more stony, chert-rich and quartzite ridges, while on the foot slopes and floors of the smaller valleys Acacia karoo joins Rhus lancea as the dominant small tree.

The floors of the larger valleys are covered by riverine gallery forest, now much disturbed by cultivation. In the undisturbed state these galleries consisted of large trees such as *Celtis kraussiana*, with a continuous crown cover and sparse undergrowth. This mosaic of different vegetation types, together with abundant water, provided an ideal environmental setting for the proliferation of a wide range of animal species (fauna), each with its particular habitat preferences. Browsing antelopes, such as modern bushbuck and kudu, prefer closed vegetation such as the riverine forests, while grazers such as impala, springbok, hartebeest and zebra prefer a grassy, savannah environment.

Top: Looking out through a cave shaft opening at Sterkfontein.
Above: The current landscape and vegetation at the Cradle of Humankind.

Wild olive indigenous to the Cradle of Humankind.

Above left: Modern lianas hanging from a tree in Mozambique. Fossil lianas found with *Australopithecus* at Sterkfontein belong to *Dichapetalum mombuttense*, a species that now occurs in the tropical forests of the Democratic Republic of the Congo and Cameroon. Above right: Remnant of gallery forest growing along the present-day Bloubank River near Sterkfontein.

As was pointed out in the Foreword to this book, more than half of the animal species found with Australopithecus africanus at Sterkfontein are now extinct, but most were related to modern species such as those listed earlier, and had similar habitat preferences.

By analysing the frequency of browsers versus grazers among the fossil remains it is possible for faunal specialists to draw broad conclusions about the patterns of vegetation in the area at the time the remains accumulated. For example, we infer that, at the time of *Australopithecus*, more than 2 million years ago, considerably more riverine forest was present in the area than is the case today because browsing antelopes are more prevalent in these deposits than in modern assemblages (other indicators are the greater abundance of forest-dwelling monkeys and the presence of the fossilised remains of lianas of the species *Dichapetalum mombuttense*, which grow only in forest habitats).

We can conclude also, on the basis of different fauna, that the vegetation had become more open by the time that *Paranthropus* and *Homo* appeared in the South African fossil record from about 2 million years ago onwards. Some researchers have argued that the emergence of these two hominid genera, and the more 'modern' animal species which accompanied them, was directly linked to pressures exerted by changing environmental circumstances on evolutionary processes; these, they maintain, led to the 'selection' of species with biological features better suited to the new habitat.

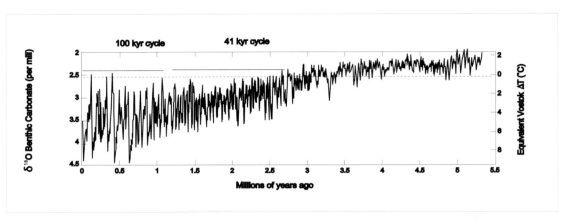

Five-million-year record of temperature change reconstructed from deep sea sediment cores by Lisiecki and Raymo in 2005. Temperature scale on right shows change in relation to the Vostok temperature datum in Antarctica.

These events were apparently driven by natural climate change: from about 2.6 million years ago a worldwide period of cooling and drying has been recognised in records from the deep oceans and other natural archives (see diagram above). In East Africa the earliest known Paranthopus is 2.5 million years old and the earliest Homo 2.3 million years.

How can we determine the age of the various fossils and the times at which major environmental changes occurred? The first prerequisite for any assessment of age is an understanding of the stratigraphy of the deposit to be dated. Stratigraphy is simply the sequence of the various layers (or strata) of which the deposit is made up, from bottom to top and from oldest to youngest. In a dolomitic cave these are not necessarily synonymous: because the cave deposits are lime-cemented and are thus soluble by rain water. Cavities can form within or below them into which younger material can be introduced from the surface through new openings to produce an inversion of stratigraphy. This has happened at Sterkfontein and Swartkrans, and probably also in most of the cave deposits of the Cradle, as is shown in the diagram on the opposite page. In such situations it is usually relatively easy to distinguish between different generations of deposits on the basis of their characteristics and entry points. It has become customary within the Cradle to number the various layers (members) in sequence from oldest to youngest as is illustrated in the figure on page 46 showing the stratigraphy at Sterkfontein.

The use of faunal comparison as a dating tool (the matching of species in the South African ape-man deposits with counterparts in the well-dated sites of East Africa) was mentioned in the Foreword to this book. Until quite recently this was the best method by which to estimate the age of the South African fossil remains; unfortunately, it could yield only rather approximate ages.

More recently, two techniques have been found to be applicable to the travertine (limestone) layers within the cave breccias; the travertines contain a little dust as well as very small traces of uranium, both of which

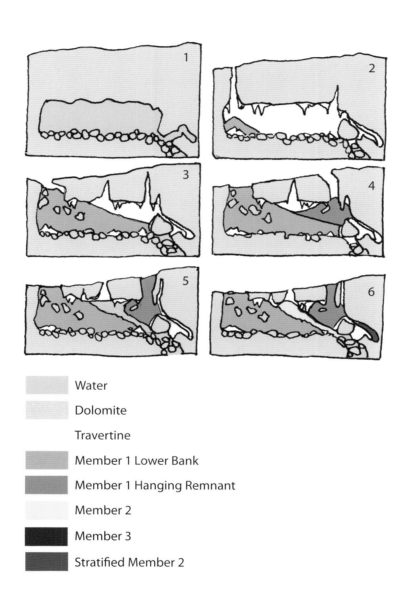

Water

Dolomite

Travertine

Member 1 Lower Bank

Member 1 Hanging Remnant

Member 2

Member 3

Stratified Member 2

Schematic sections through the Swartkrans hominid site, showing stages in the accumulation of the breccia infilling of the cave. In panels 5 and 6 note how the younger Members 2 and 3 accumulated in a solution channel dissolved within the Member 1 breccia, creating an inversion of stratigraphy in which younger deposits lie below older deposits. (After reconstructions by C.K. Brain.)

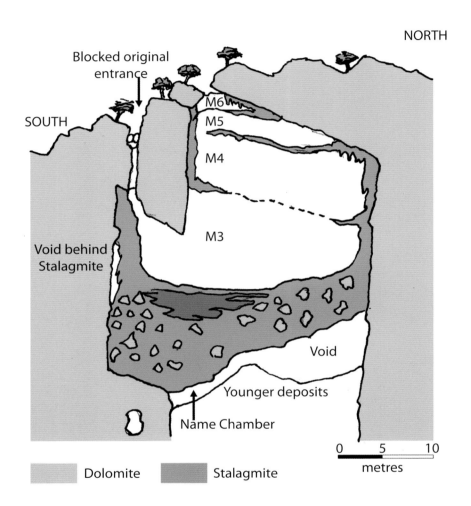

Schematic north-south section through the Sterkfontein hominid site showing the stratigraphy (sequence of Members) and the position of the suggested original opening to the cave. After illustration by Ron Clarke.

The Sterkfontein Oldowan has been dated using the cosmogenic nuclide burial method. Scientists Darryl Granger and Ryan Gibbon measured the length of time over which a quartz cobble lay buried in the deposit, calculating that this Oldowan cobble is about 2 million years old. The measurements were made at Purdue University in the USA. Isotopes of aluminum and beryllium are captured in quartz when it is exposed on the land surface. After burial the isotopes decay at known rates over time. The Oldowan cobble had been carried to the site by hominids and was contemporary with their occupation of the site.

can now be used as dating tools. The development of very precise magnetometers from the 1990s onward created the possibility of using past changes in the magnetic field of the earth to provide an age range for the fossils, through careful sampling and analysis of the dust in travertines occurring in layers above and below these specimens. The magnetic field of the earth has behaved in an unstable manner over much of geological time, undergoing relatively rapid changes from periods when the magnetic north pole was near to the true North Pole, to times when it swung by 180 degrees to near the South Pole.

The timing of these changes is well known from many measurements made on dated lava flows across the world. The record is especially good for the Neogene period spanning the past 23 million years. These results have yielded a palaeomagnetic time-scale which serves as a global yard-stick.

A problem is that any record from an undated site can be divided into two components only: periods when the magnetic pole was in the north (normal periods) and periods when it was in the south (reversed periods). If there are breaks in the sequence of deposits to be measured and these represent significant periods of time, matching the results to the world wide palaeomagnetic time-scale may allow for alternative interpretations, even when rough dating (with an accuracy usually no better than a few hundred thousand years) is available from faunal comparisons.

Another problem to be taken into account is that, as mentioned above, younger deposits can fill cavities in or below older deposits; the same is true of stalagmite flowstone, younger generations of which can penetrate into fissures in older deposits. Thus we must carefully assess the stratigraphy before applying dating methods.

Over large areas of the Bloubank River valley the natural vegetation is a sparse *Rhus*, such as the above.

At Sterkfontein application of the palaeomagnetic technique on travertine deposits by Tim Partridge and his co-workers suggested that the lower part of the cave fill (close to the bottom of Member 2), which contains the almost complete Little Foot skeleton, is between 3.30 and 3.33 million years old. Another possibility would be to place the flowstone between 3.04 and 3.11 million years. However, we now understand that the flowstone encasing the skeleton formed considerably later than the sediments, filling in gaps created by subsidence of the deposit. This is clear because the flowstone covers the upper part of the body as far as mid-thigh and then continues beneath its lower legs. Using the same palaeomagnetic method, that part of the deposit hosting Mrs Ples is best bracketed considerably later at between 2.15 and 2.14 million years; this is scarcely surprising, as Mrs Ples is almost 10 metres higher in the sequence of deposits which accumulated as the cave filled up with soil, rubble, travertine and bone remains.

The palaeomagnetic method of age estimation has been applied also by Francis Thackeray and Joe Kirschvink to the Kromdraai B site, which has yielded fossils of Paranthropus. Their results show that, within the age constraints imposed by the fossil fauna, these hominid specimens date to between 1.77 and 1.95 million years, i.e., at least 200 000 years after the time of Mrs Ples.

Recent advances in the use of the rate at which the unstable uranium isotope, U238, decays into lead have opened the possibility of obtaining absolute (i.e., unique) dates for the older cave deposits of the Cradle. This method is, like palaeomagnetism, of use only in the travertine layers within the fossil-bearing breccias. Researchers at the University of Bern in Switzerland have refined earlier results to calculate an age of between 2.8 and 2.6 million years for some Member 2 flowstones at Sterkfontein which enclose the Little

Top: Dolomite rock exposed at Sterkfontein.
Above: A cave shaft opening at the Sterkfontein Caves.

The landscape of the Cradle of Humankind at dusk and sunset.

Foot skeleton. This age is somewhat younger than that suggested by the palaeomagnetic results. However, the discrepancy could result from errors arising from the addition of more recent travertine through fissures which are present in the unstable talus cone in which this fossil is preserved. Furthermore, as noted above, flowstone which sandwiches the skeleton could only have formed after the collapse, which could have been long after the skeleton was deposited. The age range obtained for the much thicker sequence of Member 4 deposits, near the top of which Mrs Ples was found, is 2.6 to 2.0 million years, which accords well with the palaeomagnetic results.

Finally, researchers have found a new method for dating some events at Sterkfontein –cosmogenic nuclide burial dating – has recently been applied. The method is still in the experimental stage for the dating of breccias, because of the complexities of understanding the exact proportion of quartz grains entering the cave from the surface versus quartz released from the dolomite within the cave or re-worked from much older generations of cave fill. However, the results from a cobble of quartz transported to the site by hominids have produced one trustworthy result thus far, dating the earliest known artefacts in Southern Africa to about 2 million years.

The excavation site at Sterkfontein Caves.

Chapter *THREE*
NESTING IN TREES

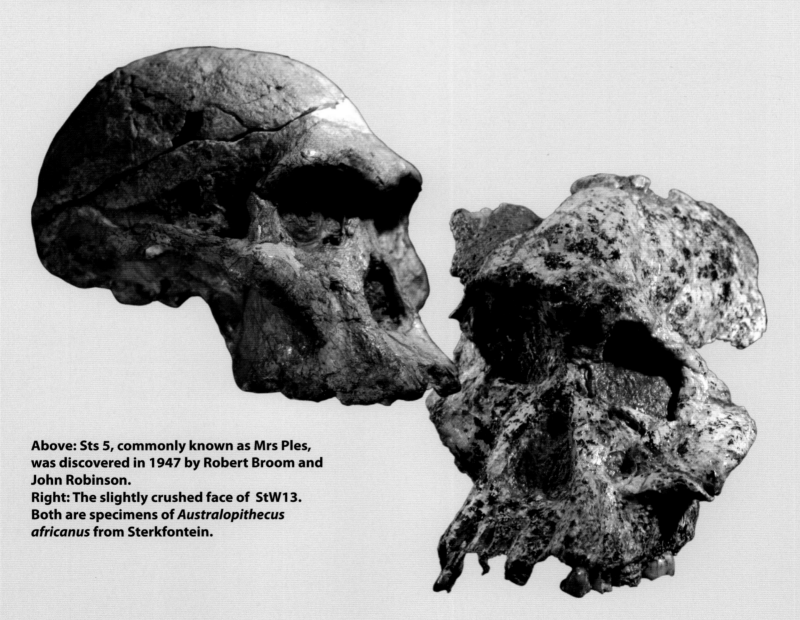

Above: Sts 5, commonly known as Mrs Ples, was discovered in 1947 by Robert Broom and John Robinson.
Right: The slightly crushed face of StW13. Both are specimens of *Australopithecus africanus* from Sterkfontein.

**R. J. Clarke's representation of an
Australopithecus africanus male.**

All of us tend to live in some kind of nest, a place of safety and comfort to sleep at night, away from predators. Nowadays, these nests are nearly always on the ground in the form of houses or huts, although there are people in some parts of the world who build their houses in trees or on platforms. The great apes of today make nests for sleeping in trees and it is most probable that the earliest ape-like human ancestors did so also. Environmental information from the sites that have produced fossil remains of these early hominids indicates that they lived in forest or woodland and that those areas were frequented also by hyaenas and large felids, such as sabre-toothed cats, lions and leopards. It would thus have aided the survival of our ancestors if they spent time in the trees.

The oldest hominids so far known are the 7 million-year-old Sahelanthropus from Chad, the 6 million-year-old Orrorin from Kenya, and Ardipithecus (at between 5.8 and 4.4 million years) from Ethiopia. The Cradle of Humankind does not have any sites with fossil hominids as old as these, but it does have the richest treasury of fossils of the best represented early hominid, Australopithecus.

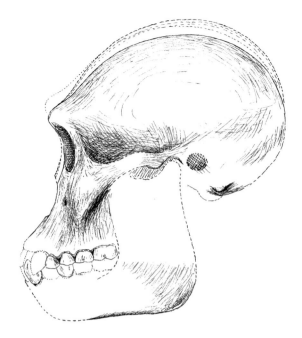

Robert Broom's reconstruction of the TM 1511 cranium with the canine of the child Sts 50 in 1946 Transvaal Museum memoir 2.

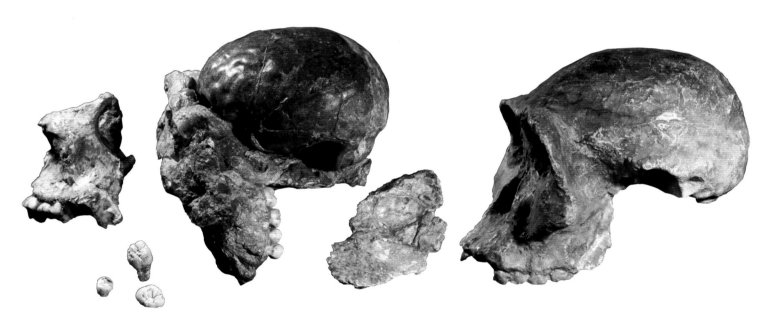

Above left: The first adult *Australopithecus* cranium TM 1511, found at Sterkfontein in 1936 by Robert Broom. Above right: Broom's reconstructed model of the cranium.

This genus, a human ancestral relative, was first recognised by Raymond Dart in 1925 after the discovery of the skull of a three– or four-year-old child at Buxton Limeworks near Taung, South Africa. He named it *Australopithecus africanus*, meaning the southern ape of Africa and observed that, although it had a small brain little larger than that of a chimpanzee, it had human-like though large cheek teeth, and a small human-like canine tooth. In 1936 Robert Broom found the first adult *Australopithecus* at Sterkfontein Caves. It was a crushed skull with an associated natural braincast, and he named it *Australopithecus transvaalensis*. Two years later at Sterkfontein, he discovered the front of a lower jaw of an ape-man child with a large canine tooth which he regarded as so different from the Taung Child that he placed it in a new genus, *Plesianthropus* (meaning near-man).

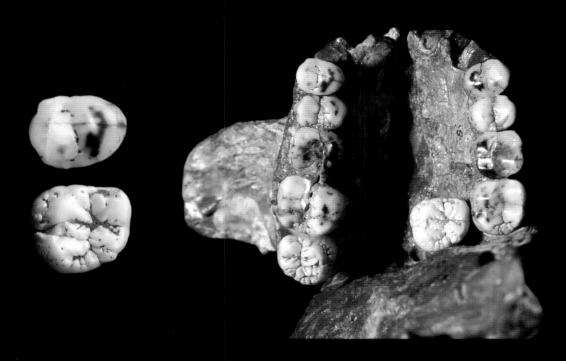

Above: In 1936 Robert Broom discovered the first adult *Australopithecus*, of which this is the palate. Two of the teeth, the left molar and the right front premolar, were identified from the lime miners' dump 66 years after Broom's discovery. These two teeth are placed on the palate, but the third molar is placed next to the second molar because its correct position is covered in matrix. The two teeth are shown separately (enlarged) on the left and match the top left tooth and bottom right tooth on the left, respectively.

Below: Two further palates of *Australopithecus africanus*, Sts53 (left) and StW53 (right). All three palates belong to *Australopithecus africanus* males.

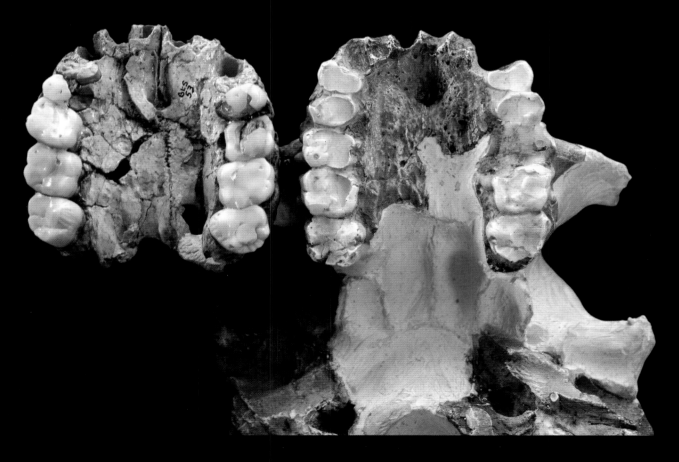

Avove left: Front view of the skull of Mrs Ples (Sts 5).
Above centre and right: The upper jaw of this female *Australopithecus africanus* (TM 1512) shows the small canine tooth, compared with the larger canine tooth in the lower face of the male (Sts 52) (above right).

In 1947 when Broom and John Robinson blasted out a well preserved adult cranium (skull), Broom proclaimed it to be an elderly female of Plesianthropus; a local newspaper named it 'Mrs Ples' for short. This was not the only cranium found at Sterkfontein, but it became well known because it was complete except for its teeth and was not crushed.

By contrast, Broom's 1936 cranium from Sterkfontein was crushed but had many of its teeth preserved. In 2002 (66 years after Broom's first discovery), Ron Clarke identified, in breccia left by lime miners in their waste dumps, two teeth of the same individual. The cranium now has all premolars and all molars represented. Several other fossils of ape-man crania, mandibles and teeth were recovered by Broom and Robinson at Sterkfontein, and Broom classified the big-toothed specimens as male and the small-toothed as female. Meanwhile, at Makapansgat in the Limpopo Province, Raymond Dart's team of Alun Hughes and the Kitching brothers were discovering similar ape-man fossils in lime mining waste dumps; the first, which came to light in 1947, was the back of a braincase, catalogued as MLD 1 (MLD stands for Makapansgat Limeworks Dumps). Also in 1947, Broom and Robinson found at Sterkfontein a partial skeleton (Sts 14) consisting of a complete pelvis, vertebral column and poorly preserved partial thigh bone. The pelvis showed conclusively that *Australopithecus* walked upright and was of short stature. It was a short, broad-bladed pelvis like that of humans and unlike the tall, narrow-bladed pelvis of apes. Two similar fragments of pelvis were recovered at Makapansgat

From 1966 onwards, Phillip Tobias and Alun Hughes began a systematic, full-time excavation at Sterkfontein that continues at present. This resulted in the recovery of a large number of *Australopithecus* fossils, including crania, mandibles, teeth and limb bones, as well as another partial skeleton, StW 431. When Ron Clarke reconstructed the fragments of one of the fossil crania, StW 252, he formed the opinion that it and several other specimens were so distinct from *Australopithecus africanus* in tooth form and size, as well as in cranial shape, that they must be considered as a second *Australopithecus* species, which is represented both at Sterkfontein and at Makapansgat. This second species was a contemporary of, but differed from, *Australopithecus africanus* in having much larger cheek teeth with low bulbous cusps, prominent cheek bones, a longer face (with the central part slightly concave), and a relatively thin brow region.

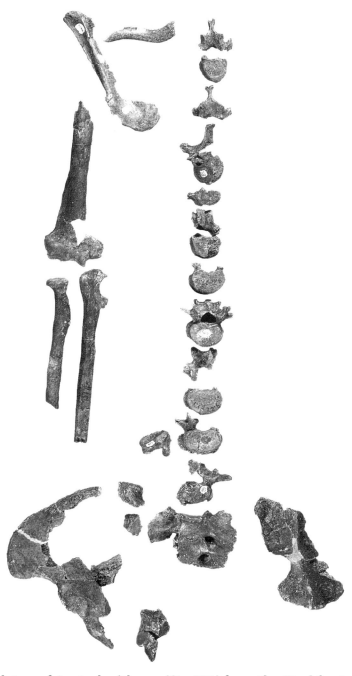

Partial skeleton of *Australopithecus* (Sts 431) from the Sterkfontein Caves.

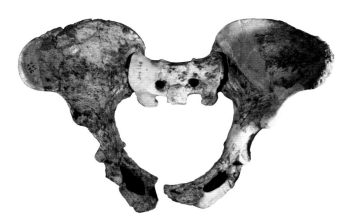

A complete reconstructed pelvis of *Australopithecus* (Sts 14) from Sterkfontein.

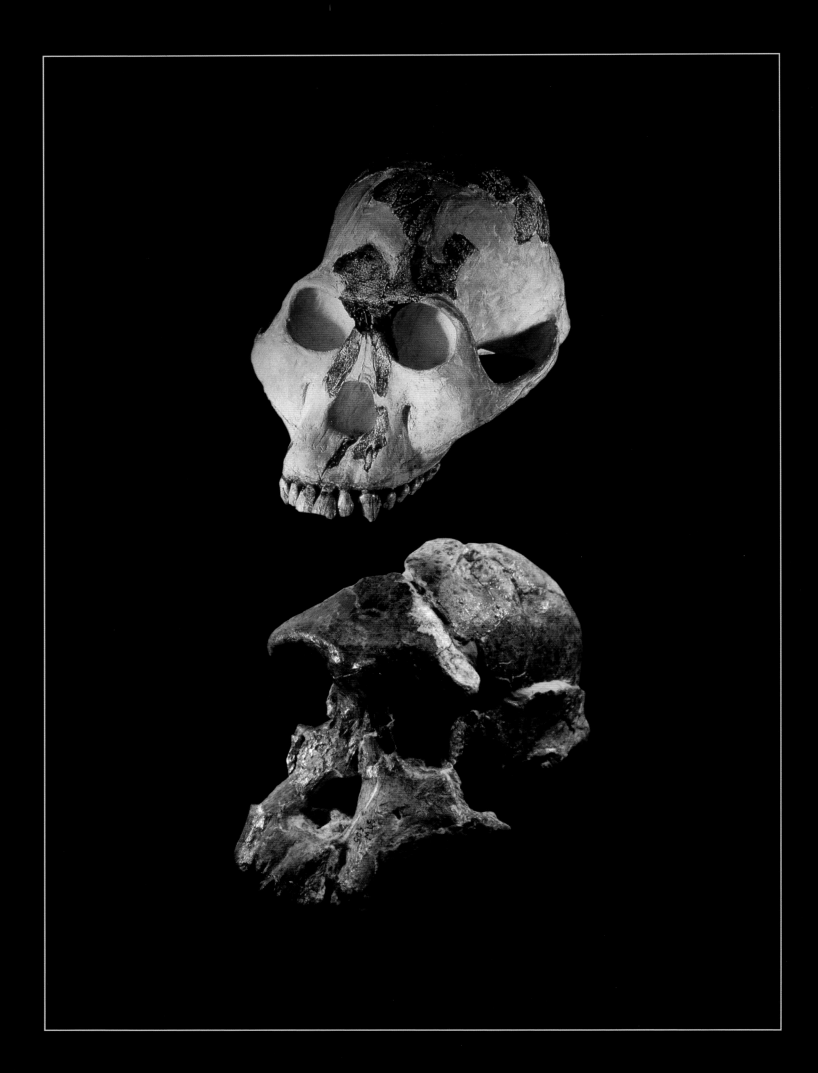

These three crania of the second *Autralopithecus* species are from a young male (StW 252) (opposite top), an old male (StW 505) (opposite bottom) and an adult female (Sts 71) (above). The low forehead with thin eyebrow ridges, the high rounded back of the skull, and the prominent cheek bones are characteristics which differentaite the second species from *Australopithecus africanus*.

These side views of a child (Taung) (top), an adult female (Sts 5) (middle), and an adult male (StW 53) (bottom) of *Australopithecus africanus* show the similarities in profile and brain size for this species of ape-man.

The middle skull (Sts 5) is Mrs Ples, the best known cranium of *Australopithecus africanus*. It was found at Sterkfontein in 1947 and dates to about 2.14 million years ago.

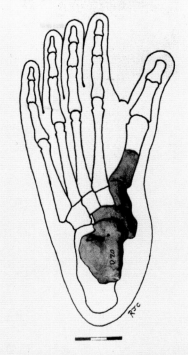

Drawing of the foot of the Little Foot skeleton by Ronald J. Clarke.

History of the Discovery of a Complete Australopithecus Skeleton, Little Foot

During the 1970s *Australopithecus* fossils were discovered at Hadar in Ethiopia and Laetoli in Tanzania in deposits going back to 3.76 million years, which makes these specimens significantly earlier than those found in South Africa. As they were even more ape-like than their South African counterparts, they were named as a new species, *Australopithecus afarensis*. There is, however, some debate as to whether the Tanzanian fossils from Laetoli should be grouped with those from Ethiopia, as the Laetoli fossils show more similarity to 4.2 million-year-old Kenyan fossils that have been named *Australopithecus anamensis*. At Laetoli the back part of a fossil hominid footprint was discovered in an exposure of volcanic tuff by Paul Abel, and subsequent excavation uncovered a trail of footprints left by two individuals walking side by side.

Although they were walking fully upright, the prints showed that the foot was not fully human and had a big toe that was slightly separated from the others. It was thus clear that this hominid could not walk as we do by using its big toe as a lever, but would have had to lift its feet as apes do when they walk on two legs.

In 1978, in the hope of finding a similarly early form of *Australopithecus* at Sterkfontein, Phillip Tobias and Alun Hughes arranged for the removal and processing of lime mining rubble from an underground cavern,

The foot had a slightly divergent big toe, which would have assisted Little Foot in tree climbing. In apes, the big toe is even more divergent, and in humans it is in line with the other toes, to facilitate toeing off during walking.
In this photograph, the upper part of the shinbone has been rejoined to its lower part and foot, which had been blasted off by lime miners.

The hand of Little Foot is like that of modern humans but much more muscular, and the arm is of similar length to the leg.

Alun Hughes (left) and Phillip Tobias (right) renewed excavations at Sterkfontein in 1966 and investigated the Silberberg Grotto breccias from 1978 to 1980.

near to the lowest part of the Sterkfontein Caves, known as the Silberberg Grotto. This cavern is named after Dr K. Silberberg, who, in the mid 1940s, collected from there a fossilised portion of a hyaena muzzle. The Abbé Breuil noticed it in Silberberg's art gallery and asked to take it to Broom, who identified it as a very ancient (Pliocene) form of hyaena, which is now called *Chasmaporthetes silberbergi*. This suggested to Broom that Sterkfontein was older than he had previously thought. The processing of the lime mining rubble from the Silberberg Grotto by Alun Hughes and his team yielded large quantities of fossils, mainly of monkeys, big cats and hyaenas, but not one tooth of a hominid.

In 1994, whilst he was looking at a box of those animal bones in the Sterkfontein store room, Ron Clarke discovered four hominid foot bones leading from the ankle to the back of the big toe; the anatomy indicated that, like the hominid that made the Laetoli footprints, it had a slightly divergent big toe.

Three years later, in a box of monkey fossils that came from the Silberberg Grotto and were stored in the Anatomy Department at the University of the Witwatersrand in Johannesburg, Clarke found more bones of the same foot and the lower end of a shin bone. He also found, among the antelope bones in the Sterkfontein store, the lower half of the other shin bone that fitted on to the left foot. Thus he had part of the left foot and lower leg, as well as the right lower shin bone, and also a partial foot bone from the right side. He reasoned that, if he had both left and right feet and lower legs, then the rest of the skeleton must still be in place in the Silberberg Grotto, where the lime miners had blasted off the rock containing the lower legs. He gave a cast of the right shin bone fragments to his assistants, Stephen Motsumi and Nkwane Molefe, and asked them to use hand-held lamps to search in the dark cave to see if they could find, exposed in the breccia, a piece of bone to which the shin bone would join.

Little Foot fell into a vertical shaft, just as many carnivores and monkeys did. The body of Little Foot lay on a steep debris slope before it was sealed in by more debris and flowstone.
Above: R. J. Clarke's representation of how Little Foot lay on the debris.
Below: The skull and upper arm bone of Little Foot.

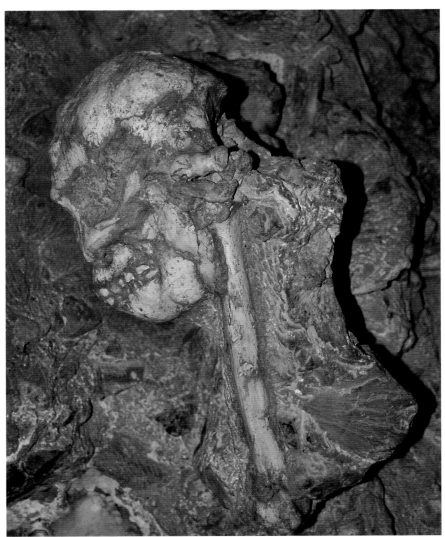

The Little Foot skeleton was discovered in 1997 in a rocky slope of Member 2 breccia, within the dark recesses of the Silberberg Grotto.

Remarkably, after only one and a half days of searching, they found a bone broken by blasting and the shin bone fragment joined to it perfectly. Subsequent excavation has exposed most of the skeleton and a complete skull. This is popularly known as Little Foot, after Phillip Tobias named the first four foot bones 'Little Foot' to contrast with the legendary 'Big Foot' of North America.

The skull of Little Foot is not like that of *Australopithecus africanus* and has more similarity to the second species of *Australopithecus* mentioned earlier. The completeness of the skeleton and lack of any sign of carnivore damage show that it must represent an individual who fell down a vertical shaft and could not have been scavenged by hyaenas. At a later date, sediment beneath the rocky debris that entombed the skeleton was washed away either by the rising water table or by water flowing down the debris slope. This left a shallow cavity into which the central part of the skeleton collapsed. This collapse caused breakage and displacement of many elements of the skeleton. Calcareous flowstone (stalagmite) then formed over the upper part of the skeleton but then continued beneath its lower legs.

It can be seen that, in spite of the breakage, the arms and legs of Little Foot are of approximately equal length. This differs from modern humans, in which legs are longer than arms, and from apes in which arms are longer than legs. The hand is of particular interest because, although much more muscular, it is proportioned like that of humans, with a short palm and fingers but a long thumb. Such a hand is primitive in form and designed for branch grasping whilst climbing in trees, and is unlike the specialised ape hand which has a long palm and fingers and a short thumb. The ape's hand is thus able to form a hook for suspending the body beneath branches.

The relatively short arm and human-like hand with a long thumb are designed for tree climbing by branch grasping and is an ancestral condition. Apes, by contrast, have specialised long arms and hands for suspension by swinging beneath branches. When they come to the ground they use the long arms as supports for walking (knuckle or fist walking).

The anatomy of the *Australopithecus* arm and hand confirms that our ancestors did not pass through such a long-armed knuckle-walking stage. The branch grasping hand possessed by our ancestors was to prove

R. J. Clarke's drawings of males (left) and females (right) of the three species of ape-men found in the Cradle of Humankind. From top to bottom: *Australopithecus africanus;* second species of *Australopithecus;* and *Paranthropus.*

useful by about 2.6 million years ago for the manipulation of stones in order to make and use the earliest stone tools. In fact, we owe our success as cultural human beings to the tree climbing adaptability of our hand anatomy.

It is known that *Australopithecus africanus* existed at Sterkfontein until just over 2 million years ago (Chapter 2). As the earliest known *Homo* fossil from Ethiopia is 2.34 million years old, it seems that *Australopithecus* did not disappear once *Homo* had evolved. In Bed I at Olduvai Gorge in Tanzania, in the period from about 1.9 million years ago, *Homo habilis* and an *Australopithecus* with affinities to *Australopithecus africanus* co-existed and were contemporary, also, with *Paranthropus boisei*. At Lake Turkana in Kenya, *Homo ergaster*, *Paranthropus boisei* and a form of *Australopithecus* with similarities to *Australopithecus africanus* were also contemporaries.

Thus Australopithecus africanus and the second, bigger-toothed, species of Australopithecus at Sterkfontein can be considered as close ancestral relatives of humans, rather than direct ancestors.

An account of the fossil animals that shared the environment of *Australopithecus* is provided in Chapter 6.

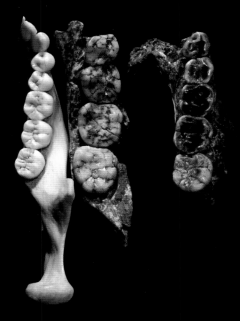

The teeth in the *Australopithecus africanus* mandible (StW 404) (right), are compared to the much larger teeth of the second species in the jaw (StW 384) (centre). The teeth of a modern human (left) are dwarfed by the massive molars and premolars of the second species.

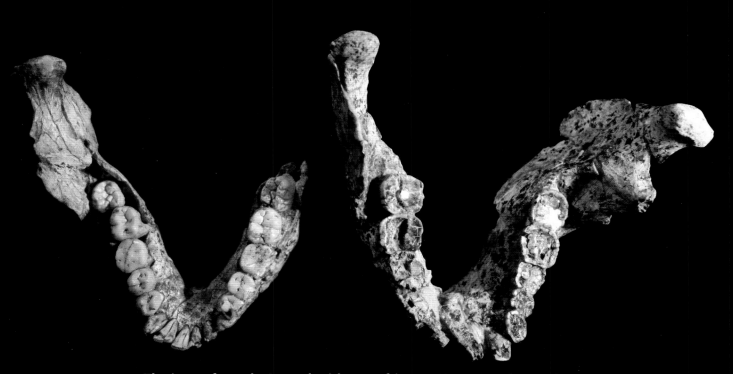

The jaws of a male *Australopithecus africanus* (Sts 52) and a much larger mandible (Sts 36) which belongs to the second species of *Australopithecus*. The two were contemporary with one another.

Chapter FOUR
CHEWERS OF ROOTS

Above and right: One of the best known crania of *Paranthropus* (SK 48), which shows the flat face, the slightly depressed forehead region, the ribs over the eye sockets and the crest on top of the skull.

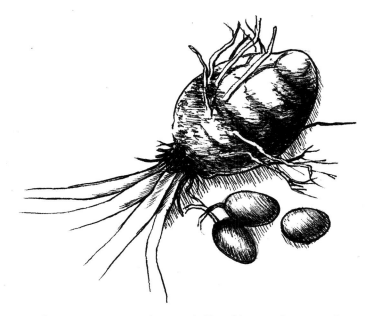

***Paranthropus* apparently specialised in crushing and grinding hard foods, such as this African potato tuber (Hypoxis), as well as roots, seeds and hard berries, with its teeth.**

The Bizarre Flat-Faced Ape-Men of the Cradle

On the 8th of June 1938, whilst on a visit to Sterkfontein, Robert Broom was shown a fossil ape-man palate by the quarry manager. The palate had one first molar tooth in position and Broom could see that the ape-man to which it belonged differed from the Sterkfontein ape-man. He gave the manager £2 for the palate, but, as the adhering breccia differed from that of Sterkfontein, he suspected that it did not come from there. On the following Saturday, when he knew the manager would be absent, he went to Sterkfontein again and showed the palate to the quarry workers, who said that they had not seen it before. On the following Tuesday Broom again went to Sterkfontein and insisted on being told how the fossil had been obtained. The manager then recounted that it had been given to him by a schoolboy, Gert Terblanche, who lived about two miles away. Broom set off for Gert's home and met his mother and sister, who told him that Gert was at school and that he had four beautiful teeth with him. The sister showed Broom where Gert had found the fossil in an ancient cave infill on a nearby hill at Kromdraai; there Broom picked up some fragments of the skull.

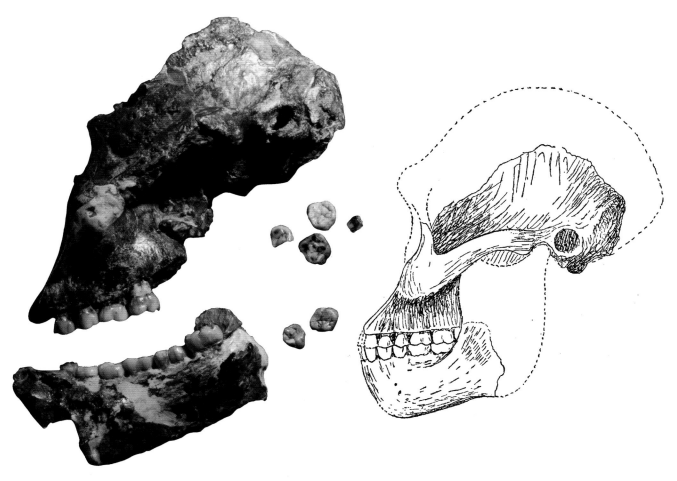

Above left: The first discovery of a *Paranthropus* was this partial skull from Kromdraai B, found in 1938.
Above right: Robert Broom's side view of the Kromdraai ape-man, *Paranthropus robustus*, 1950.

He then went to the school where the headmaster found Gert; Broom records that the boy 'drew from the pocket of his trousers four of the most wonderful teeth ever seen in the world's history.' Broom promptly purchased them from Gert and found that two of them, a premolar and molar, fitted on to the palate. Broom gave a lecture to the 120 children and four teachers about caves and fossils until school finished for the day. Gert then took Broom to the site and showed him a lower jaw that he had hidden there.

After Broom had cleaned and joined all the fragments of the skull he had much of the face and palate and part of the braincase, as well as the right side of the lower jaw. In sum, it differed from the Sterkfontein ape-men in that the teeth were larger, the jaw was more powerful, and the face was flatter. He named it as a new genus and species, *Paranthropus robustus*, implying that it was parallel to the human line and was robustly structured.

Many of the Swartkrans fossils, such as this big male cranium (SK 83), have been crushed by rockfall. The top picture shows how a large rock could have crushed in the top of the braincase.

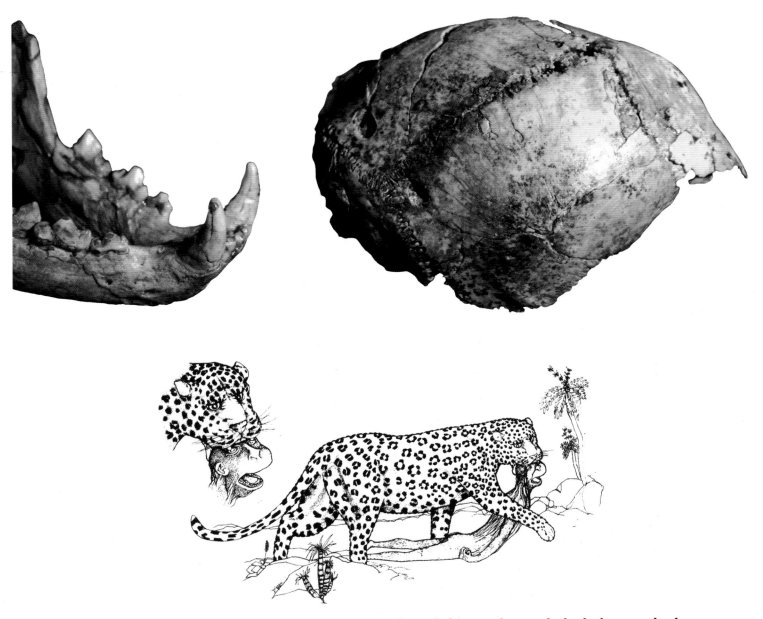

The canine teeth of the Swartkrans fossil leopard (top left) exactly match the holes punched through the braincase of the infant *Paranthropus* (SK 54) (top right).
Above: Illustration of leopard holding the *Paranthropus*, courtesy of C.K. Brain.

CHEWERS OF ROOTS

Just how unique and specialised Paranthropus was would become clear only from 1948 onwards when Broom and John Robinson recovered large numbers of Paranthropus fossils from the Swartkrans cave, a kilometre to the west of Sterkfontein. There they found many massive jaws and flat-faced skulls, some of which had a bony crest running along the top midline of the skull for the anchoring of the huge muscles needed for the operation of such massive chewing equipment.

The cheek teeth differed from those of *Australopithecus*, not only in being larger, but also in having lower, more bulbous cusps. These latter were commonly worn to a flat chewing surface, across which numerous scratches extended from side to side. This hominid apparently specialised in crushing and grinding hard foods such as roots and hard berries with its teeth. In order to facilitate the side to side grinding action of the jaws, the canine and incisor teeth were much reduced in size and appeared to be crowded in a small space between the greatly enlarged premolars. *Paranthropus* also has a very characteristic forehead region which, instead of rising upward behind the brows, is slightly concave and is bounded on either side by the bony lines marking the attachments for the jaw muscles. These massive muscles constricted the brain case behind the brow region so that the brow ridges form ribs extending over the upper sides of the eye sockets. The surface of the bone beneath the nose runs smoothly into the floor of the nasal cavity. This feature differs from that in *Australopithecus* and *Homo*, where there is a marked division between the floor of the nose and the facial surface below.

The strange structure of the skull of Paranthropus is the result of an emphasis on large grinding teeth, with correspondingly massive jaw muscles. In order to make room behind it for these enlarged muscles the cheek bone has moved so far forward that it protrudes beyond the bones of the nose. This gives the face a characteristic saucer shape.

This feature does not exist in *Australopithecus* or *Homo* because of the forward position of the nose relative to the cheek bones. John Robinson, who worked as Broom's assistant on the *Paranthropus* fossils, remarked that *Paranthropus* could be distinguished from *Australopithecus* 'by means of almost any bits of skeleton now known in both forms' and noted further that the large grinding teeth indicated such a high degree of dietary specialisation that it was justified to classify *Paranthropus* as a genus entirely distinct from *Australopithecus*.

An answer to the conundrum of why so many *Paranthropus* fossils occur at Swartkrans was provided by Bob Brain when he noted that a child *Paranthropus* braincase (SK 54) had two small holes punched through it that matched the tips of the canines of the lower jaw of a leopard. This suggested to him that leopards were largely responsible for accumulating the *Paranthropus* remains.

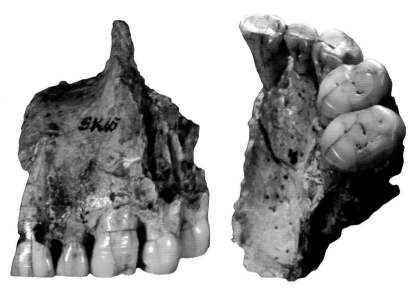

Two views of the lower facial fragment of the male *Paranthropus* (SK 65) show the small incisors and canines (left) next to the expanded premolars (right).

Found also at Swartkrans were a few other hominid fossils; these were unlike Paranthropus and much more akin to humans. Broom and Robinson named them Telanthropus capensis. They considered this form to be 'true man', which lived at the same time as the ape-man Paranthropus. These specimens, which are now generally classified as Homo ergaster, are considered further in Chapter 5, which deals with ancient stone tools. The fact that there are so few of them, compared to the abundant Paranthropus fossils, suggests that they were able to avoid falling prey to carnivore attacks and perhaps used fire to safeguard themselves at night.

In July 1959 Mary Leakey discovered the cranium of a more massive variant of *Paranthropus* in Bed I of Olduvai Gorge in Tanzania; this was dated later to 1.75 million years ago by the potassium-argon method (see Chapter 1). It was at first named *Zinjanthropus boisei*, but it is now classified as *Paranthropus boisei* and represents a more massive, East African version of the flat-faced, big-toothed genus from South Africa. Subsequent excavation revealed that the *Zinjanthropus* cranium was associated with a widespread scatter of crude stone artefacts (choppers, cores and flakes of the Oldowan Industry) and broken animal bones. Nowadays it is considered that *Paranthropus* was so specialised that it was probably not the maker of these tools, but that the contemporary *Homo habilis* made them and broke up the bones. Leakey's was the first of many discoveries of *Paranthropus* in East Africa, from sites at Peninj (Tanzania), Chesowanja and Lake Turkana (Kenya), and Omo and Konso (Ethiopia), as well as Malema in Malawi. Among these fossils was a partial female cranium, KNM ER 732 from East Lake Turkana, which showed that the females, although much smaller, had the typical *Paranthropus* flat face, emphasis on large cheek teeth, and extreme constriction of the brain case behind the eye sockets, but lacked the crest on top of the brain case.

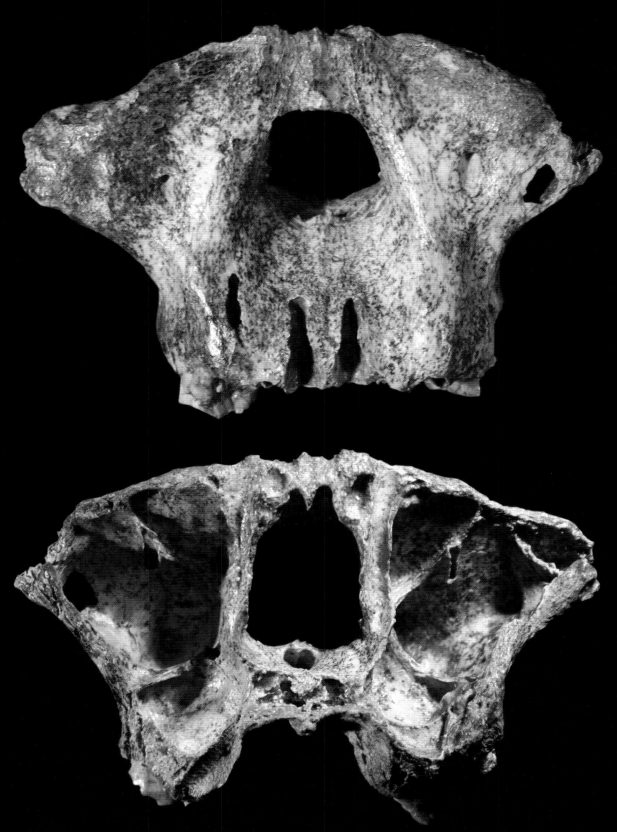

Top: The front view of a massive male *Paranthropus* lower face (SK12) shows the flatness of the face and the smooth slope of the bone running into the floor of the nose. **Bottom:** An internal view of the back of the face illustrates the capacious maxillary sinuses.

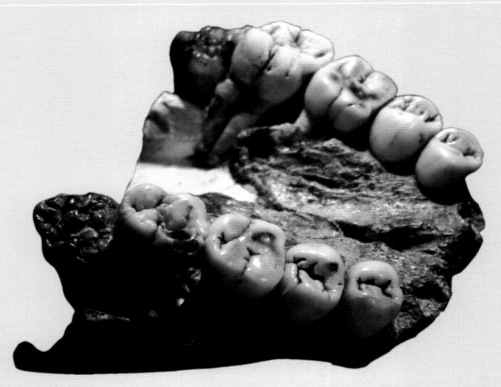

From Omo in Ethiopia comes the earliest known species of Paranthropus , dating to about 2.6 million years ago. It was first named Paraustralopithecus aethiopicus, but is now classed as Paranthropus aethiopicus and is grouped together with a 2.5 million year old complete cranium, lacking teeth, which was found at Lomekwi on the west side of Lake Turkana in Kenya. This cranium (KNM WT 17000), known as the Black Skull because of its colour, had a larger space for teeth in the front of its jaw than is found in the later species of Paranthropus.

The brain size of *Paranthropus* was about 500 to 530 cc, which is larger than that of *Australopithecus*; this is probably related to its larger body size. The *Paranthropus*-rich site of Swartkrans has fossil deposits that date back to about 2 million years ago and is approximately equivalent in age to Member 5 of Sterkfontein. Although the two sites are a short distance apart on opposite sides of the Bloubank River, they differ markedly in their *Paranthropus* content. Swartkrans has abundant *Paranthropus* fossils, whilst Sterkfontein Member 5 has only a few teeth which are associated with the Oldowan Industry; no *Paranthropus* remains are associated with the Early Acheulean Industry. There are also very few *Paranthropus* fossils from the Cooper's site and from Kromdraai B, which are both on the same side of the river as Sterkfontein, whilst abundant *Paranthropus* fossils were recovered from Drimolen, which is on the Swartkrans side, although much further away. From Drimolen came the first complete skull (cranium plus lower jaw) of a female *Paranthropus*. One large *Paranthropus* molar has also been recovered at the site of Gondolin, in the far north of the Cradle. These differences in the distribution of *Paranthropus* remains might be explained by differences in the ages of the sites, by environmental preferences of the hominids, or by patterns of predation.

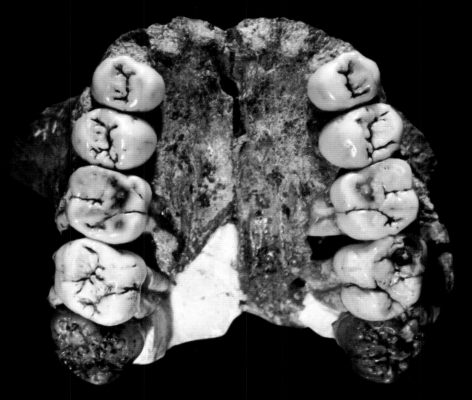

Above and left: Two views of the palate of *Paranthropus* (SK 13) show the large, bulbous cheek teeth with flat grinding surfaces and the restricted space for the canines and incisors.

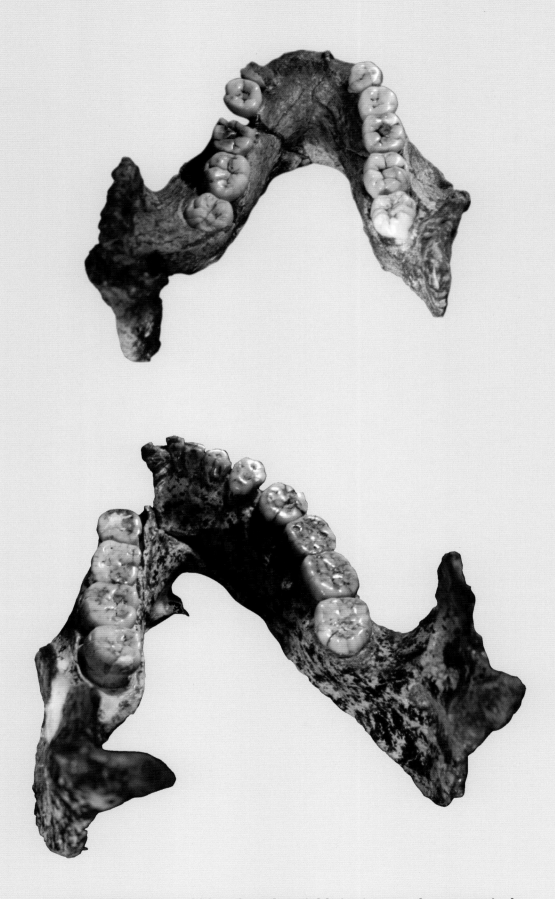

The *Paranthropus* mandibles, though variable in size, are always massively constructed and have large cheek teeth. A small mandible (SKW 5) (top), compared to a very large mandible (SK 34) (above).

CHEWERS OF ROOTS

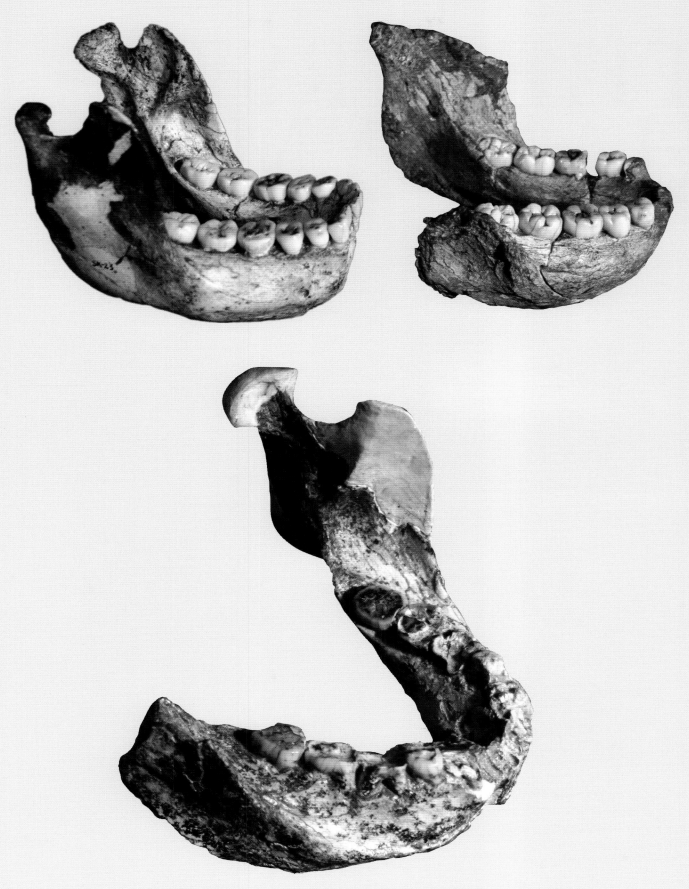

The three jaws of *Paranthropus* are the beautifully preserved (SK 23) (top left), the small mandible (SKW 5) (top right), and the massive (SK 12) (above).

Chapter FIVE

THE FIRST HANDYMEN

**Above: Oldowan cores from Sterkfontein shown
with hands to indicate actual size.**
**Above right: Oldowan core tool from Sterkfontein
shown actual size.**

CENTIMETRES

R. J. Clarke's representation of a *Homo habilis* male.

Early Cultural Origins within the Cradle

The earliest stone tools in the world, found in Ethiopia, are almost 2.6 million years old. They are flakes struck from cobbles by using another cobble as a hammer stone. These simple tools were probably fashioned to help early humans cut meat from carcasses, as bones with cut marks appear equally early in the archaeological record. Our human ancestors, like modern apes, undoubtedly used other, perishable materials in the natural world as tools, but stone tools alone provide durable evidence for the earliest human cultural behaviour.

Archaeologists study artefacts from individual sites for the technological and behavioural information which they provide, and they classify them into industries related to each other in space and time. The earliest known tools belong to the Oldowan Industry, named after important discoveries in Olduvai Gorge, Tanzania. From just after 2.6 million years ago to about 2 million years, we distinguish an 'early Oldowan' phase of tool making, while assemblages dating around 1.9 to 1.7 million years are considered a 'classic Oldowan' phase. New dates for the Oldowan stone tools from Sterkfontein suggest that they belong to the early phase of the Oldowan industry and are about 2 million years in age.

An Oldowan core in quartzite from Sterkfontein.

Oldowan tools show that their hominid makers were intelligent. They were able to select the better kinds of rocks to flake and very often detached many flakes from the same cobble. At times they carried their cobbles and flakes for some distance across the landscape.

The Sterkfontein Oldowan industry is dominated by artefacts made of vein quartz, a rock the toolmakers selected mainly from river gravels near to the site. Quartz is not the most common rock in the gravels, but it is of better quality than the quartz weathering out of the dolomite close to the cave. Quartz is brittle, comes in various sizes, and is easy to break regardless of the shape of the piece. It also makes extremely sharp flakes which are good for cutting tasks and for butchery.

Because substantial quantities of small flaking debris, typical of on-site tool making, are present, it is clear that the Oldowan tool makers worked the quartz near to the cave entrance. In contrast, the paucity of small flaking debris in quartzite suggests that most of this material was worked off-site and brought in as flakes or partly worked cores. Quartzite may have been used for tasks that required a less brittle working edge; this reveals a degree of selective skill that was clearly well within the capabilities of the Oldowan hominids.

Archaeologists study even the tiniest chips of waste left behind at a site to reconstruct the behaviour of hominids and especially to understand what natural processes may have later altered the original assemblage of worked stone left by the hominids. The quartz artefacts in the Sterkfontein Oldowan industry represent a near-complete flaking assemblage, left in the course of multiple visits to the site by hominids; only the smallest fraction of material under 10 mm size is, in fact, missing. The same is true for the small number of chert artefacts in the assemblage. These were flaked on-site, probably from solid layers of chert protruding from the dolomite, since no chert cores have been found. There is evidence for the presence of a significant amount of closed vegetation around the cave entrance (see Chapter 2); this helped to trap and retain the small flaking debris. Hominid activities took place on the surface under the shade of trees growing around cave entrances, which took the form of vertical shafts with steep drops into the caverns below. Debris from repeated occupations accumulated around such cave entrances; during the Oldowan most of it found its way into the underground cavern.

CENTIMETRES

Oldowan cores were basic but produced effective tools. Some cores were undoubtedly used for their sharp edges, but the detachment of flakes was the primary goal. Overall, Oldowan artefacts suggest a planned but casual and expedient use of stone.

During the Oldowan occupation lush vegetation grew around a narrow cave entrance. Trees provided shade for the hominids, who worked and rested there. With time, their artefacts washed into the cave shaft. The stable land surface around the shaft allowed most of the artefacts to be washed into the cave below. However, many animals that ventured there fell into the shaft as most of the fauna represents a deathtrap accumulation at the bottom of the drop. Even in today's drier landscape (pictured above), trees and bush often obscure steep shafts that lead into underground caves.

The Oldowan hominids at Sterkfontein preferred to use quartz, a brittle rock that is easy to break. It also makes very sharp edges that are good for cutting. These are flakes and debris from a quartz core worked in experiments.

In the 1960s a Shangilla man at Lake Turkana in Kenya was observed, by Ron Clarke and others, using stone tools to scavenge meat from a lion kill. He first flaked a cobble into a chopper to remove the limb of the antelope and to skin it. He then made a fresh flake to continue the skinning and broke the bone with the chopper to access the marrow. Experiments at Sterkfontein have shown that it is possible to butcher an entire antelope by using a handful of small but sharp flakes.

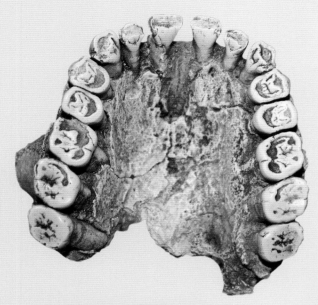

Homo habilis OH65 maxilla.

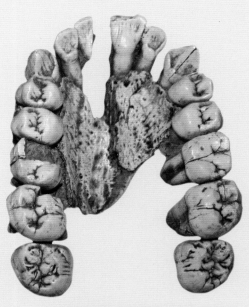

Australopithecus StW 252 maxilla.

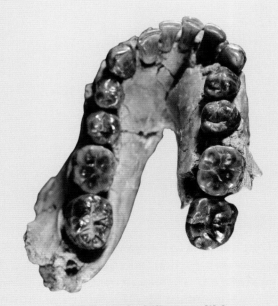

OH7 Homo habilis mandible.

Who made the Oldowan tools?

This crushed mandible, from Olduwai Gorge, Tanzania (OH7, above centre), is part of the type specimen of what Leakey, Tobias and Napier named Homo habilis, or 'handy man', the first maker of stone tools. The bones from the top of the braincase (the parietal bones) showed that it had a much larger brain than Australopithecus; hence all later finds attributed to Homo habilis should be defined by an enlarged cranial capacity, as well as smaller teeth. The palate and teeth of OH65 (top left) are compared with Australopithecus (top right), from Sterkfontein, to illustrate their more human-like shape and size.

**1470 fossil from East Lake Turkana, Kenya,
and the OH65 maxilla.**

**R. J. Clarke's representation of a female
Homo habilis.**

Some anthropologists believe that 1470 Man (above left) from East Lake Turkana, Kenya, belongs to *Homo habilis*, because of its similarly larger brain. Its nasal skeleton projects like that of humans and is unlike the flat, ape-like nose of *Australopithecus* and *Paranthropus*. Its lower face is broad and relatively flat, a characteristic shared by OH 65, shown below 1470 for comparison, and which likewise has been assigned to *Homo habilis*. Some archaeologists believe that *Paranthropus* may have made Oldowan tools, but this is debated because that genus was highly specialised and became extinct around a million years ago – an unlikely end for an adaptable, tool-using hominid. It is possible that an evolved species of *Australopithecus* could have made stone tools, but early *Homo* is found as early as 2.3 million years ago and is the most likely candidate.

CENTIMETRES

Oldowan quartz flakes from Sterkfontein were small but sharp and
highly effective cutting tools.

At Sterkfontein the Oldowan was excavated from deep levels in Member 5 East (right). Picks and jack hammers are used to remove the calcified deposits (left). The high degree of cementation permits a steep sided excavation without support but makes it difficult to maintain straight excavation faces. Individual specimens were, however, accurately positioned using the grid of wires set up for the purpose.

Most animals preserved in the Oldowan deposit fell down a steep shaft, accumulating as a death-trap assemblage. To sum up, the Sterkfontein Oldowan is similar to other early Oldowan assemblages in Africa. The technology was simple but intelligent, representing a successful way of life that lasted almost a million years.

While a few fossils of *Paranthropus* are associated with the Sterkfontein Oldowan, it is more likely that the artefacts were made by *Homo habilis*, which was a less specialised, more adaptable species that eventually gave rise to other early forms of *Homo*.

The next phase of cultural development, the Early Acheulean, is also represented at Sterkfontein, as well as in other Cradle of Humankind sites such as Kromdraai A and Swartkrans (in Members 2 and 3). Deposits containing this industry date from about 1.7 to 1.4 million years ago both in East Africa (Ethiopia, Kenya and Tanzania) and in South Africa (in the Vaal River basin). Handaxes, cleavers and other heavy duty tools such as picks make their first appearance in this industry. The early handaxes were clearly designed to have a robust tip, while cleavers were fashioned to provide a broad, strong cutting edge.

Picks may have served a similar function to handaxes, as many early handaxes are quite pick-like in form. These large cutting tools were always a minor component of any assemblage, since small flake tools continued to be made in abundance. Nevertheless, they do reflect the importance of robust cutting, chopping, hacking and digging activities to hominids that were by now more dependent on artefacts for their survival. Tasks made possible by such tools included heavy duty wood working and butchery and, possibly, digging for roots. Some East African sites of the same age also show greater concentrations of artefacts, along with large

CENTIMETRES

Picks were heavy tools that needed only a serviceable pointed end. This example is from Swartkrans.

numbers of manuports (or foreign stone cobbles carried in from elsewhere). This is a pattern which exists also at Sterkfontein. While handaxes and cleavers are the most carefully shaped of the tools, they are highly variable in form and thus un-standardised, which is typical of the Early Acheulean. The occasional piece is nevertheless quite skillfully made, which reveals the manual and mental abilities of the species.

The Acheulean deposits at Sterkfontein, Swartkrans and Kromdraai are thus far dated only on the basis of their associated fauna, which gives less precise ages than absolute dating; these sites are nonetheless valuable archives. Of special note is the fact that fossils of Homo ergaster are present in these deposits at both Sterkfontein and Swartkrans, providing the most direct association in Africa between this hominid species and the Early Acheulean.

The animal fossils from Sterkfontein indicate that the environment had, by now, become more open, probably as a result of decreasing rainfall. As artefacts accumulated on the surface around the cave entrance they were exposed to the elements, and most of the lighter pieces were eroded away by occasional heavy rains. The Sterkfontein Acheulean assemblage therefore lacks small flaking debris and is, instead, dominated by cores, manuports, and larger chunks and flakes. However, the many cores and manuports indicate that this was a long-term accumulation at a venue that was used repeatedly. If the smaller material had been preserved, the density of artefacts would have been very high. Quartzite had also become the preferred raw material at Sterkfontein, presumably because of its less brittle working edges and better ability to yield large flakes.

CENTIMETRES

Early Acheulean handaxes are simple in manufacture but are sometimes quite elegant when made on large flakes (as in the example above, shown in three views). This example is from Swartkrans, retrieved from lime mining dumps.

The Swartkrans site is important because it has yielded several generations of stone tools spanning almost 1.7 million years.

Sterkfontein is by far the most informative site for the early Acheulean Industry in the Cradle of Humankind. The Kromdraai A assemblage is small, with only one pick and no handaxes or cleavers found as yet. Swartkrans has more material of varied sizes, but it appears to have been more sporadically washed into the cave opening, and the few handaxes and cleavers found thus far come from the dumps of the early lime miners. Nevertheless, the caves at Swartkrans preserve valuable evidence of this important stage in the evolution of human behaviour.

Only one open air site is known in the Cradle of Humankind which belongs to the Early Acheulean; this is situated on the grounds of the Maropeng visitor centre. From their form and lack of sophistication, the Maropeng artefacts appear to be at least 1 million years old, but as the tools are contained in a reworked slope deposit they are unfortunately undatable. The archaeological material was concentrated on the surface during long periods of erosion and was then swept into a topographic depression in the landscape. No fauna is preserved at this site.

After about 1 million years ago Acheulean sites in Africa become increasingly numerous, with evidence for technological improvements in the production of large cutting tools at East African sites such Gadeb in Ethiopia, Olorgesailie in Kenya, and Olduvai Gorge in Tanzania. The South African record may show a similar trend, but it suffers from poor dating for sites that may fall within the last 1 million years. However, in the Vaal River basin at Barkly West (near Kimberley in the Northern Cape), we are beginning to close this

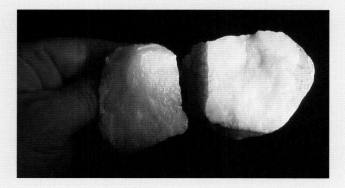

How do we recognise a stone tool?

Flakes can be struck off a cobble by hitting it between two stones – the bipolar technique (top and middle). Such flakes have a flatter inner surface and some crushing at one or both ends. In contrast, flakes struck from a cobble held in the hand are done with a freehand technique (above bottom). They have a well developed 'bulb of percussion' on the inner flake surface, produced by the force of the blow, with a corresponding hollow on the flaked rock, which is called the core. Both the bipolar (hammer and anvil) and the freehand techniques were used at Sterkfontein.

Ron Clarke at the top of a cave shaft at Sterkfontein.

gap with excavations at the site of Canteen Kopje, where quartz in cobbles and sediments can be dated by the cosmogenic nuclide burial method.

By 0.5 million years ago Acheulean sites in Africa had become widespread, reflecting the adaptive success of the evolving *Homo* lineage, despite the relatively unchanging nature of the toolkit through time. One can, however, contrast early Acheulean handaxes and cleavers, with their rough forms and bold hard-hammer shaping scars, to later Acheulean tools that are more extensively shaped, often finished with soft wood hammers to create finer cutting edges. Such technological developments, along with an increase in the number of archaeological sites, suggest that a slower, more modern rate of maturation had evolved in *Homo* by later Acheulean times. Stated differently, an extended period of juvenile development was a pre-requisite for the more evolved level of technical skill that appeared during the later Acheulean (*ca* 0.6 to 0.3 million years ago). A very adaptable, successful species had evolved.

By 200,000 to 160,000 years ago, modern *Homo sapiens* had become firmly established in the fossil record. However, archaeology suggests that the evolution of our own successful species was a process that started during later Acheulean times and continued into the early Middle Stone Age from 300,000 years ago. This was indeed a continuum, rather than an event, during which tools became lighter and technology became more varied and complex over time, with an increasing pace of change as the Middle Stone Age progressed.

While the middle and later stages of Acheulean development are not preserved at known Cradle of Humankind sites, there is good evidence that Middle Stone Age hominids were present at Plover's Lake, Sterkfontein and Swartkrans. At Swartkrans, Middle Stone Age artefacts made by modern humans accumulated on open ground near to an eastern entrance to the cave. New research by Morris Sutton shows that the assemblage is well preserved and is largely fresh, and raw materials were selected with care.

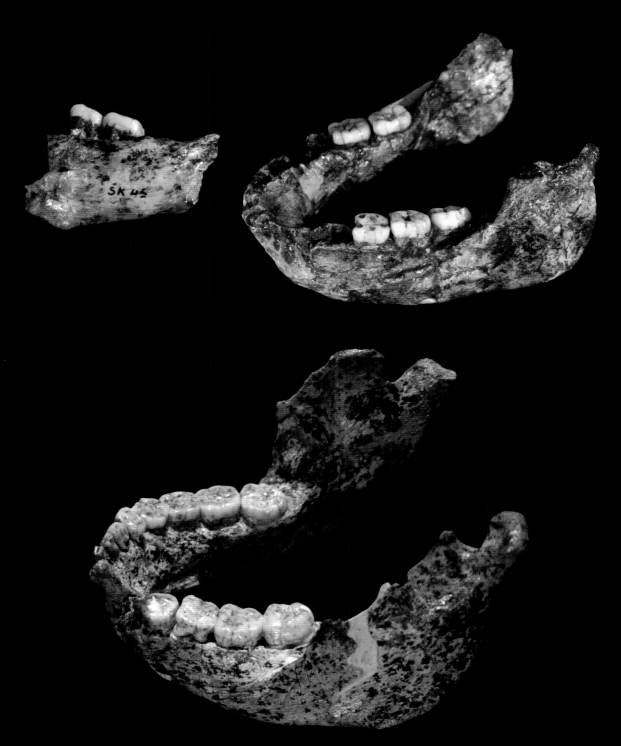

Paranthropus is present also in Members 2 and 3 at Swartkrans, but it was not a maker of Acheulean tools. *Homo ergaster* mandibles, SK 45 and SK 15 (top), are considerably less robust and more human than the massive, specialised jaws of *Paranthropus* SK 34 (bottom).

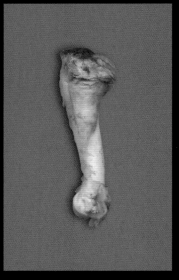
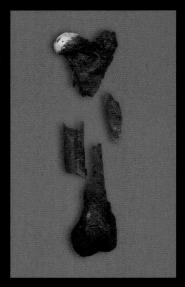
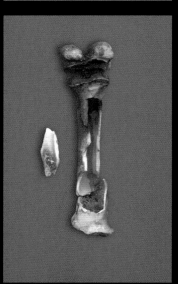
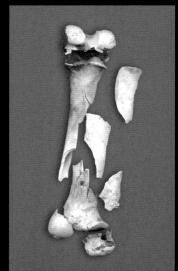

Did hominids in the Cradle of Humankind use fire?

Arguments have been advanced that hominids in East African sites were controlling fire by about 1.5 million years ago, but the evidence is not clear-cut. C.K. Brain argued that some bones in Swartkrans Member 3 (about 1 million years old) had been burnt in camp fires because they exhibit colour changes that correspond with those caused by high heat (315-480°C or more). Sustained heating in camp fires, rather than intense but rapid burning in natural bush fires, is needed to produce such changes. Megan Hanson demonstrated such colour changes with naturalistic experiments in camp fires, providing support for Brain's experiments conducted in a pottery kiln. The changes in colour are produced by the charring of carbon in the bone. Clear evidence for hearths sustained as camp fires is apparent only in the archaeological record about a half million years later.

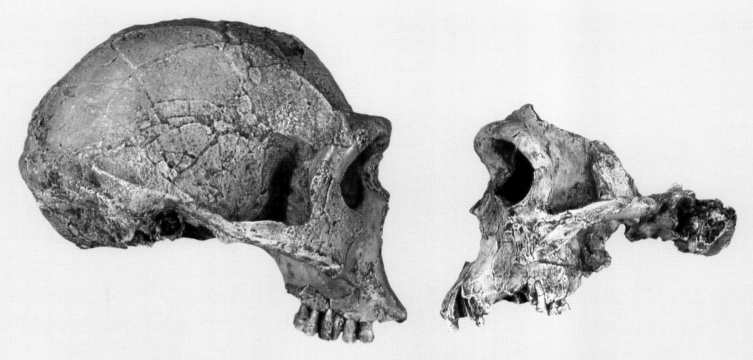

Who made the Early Acheulean tools?

Homo ergaster was larger-brained than Homo habilis and had body proportions similar to modern humans. Some researchers refer to Homo erectus as the maker of the Acheulean, but in our view that species originated in Asia and has some features that are more primitive than in Homo ergaster. The first discovery of a fossil of Homo ergaster was at Swartkrans, in the Member 1 Hanging Remnant. Here a cast of the Swartkrans specimen (SK 847, above right) is compared with a cast of the most complete cranium of the species yet found, which comes from Kenya (KNM ER 3733, above left).

Traditionally, the Middle Stone Age has been defined as a complex of industries lacking handaxes and cleavers, with an emphasis on light, portable tools. Some flakes and retouched pieces were mounted in hafts to create composite tools such as stone-tipped spears.

Although cores in some Acheulean assemblages (e.g., at Canteen Kopje) were shaped in a standardised way with careful preparation to produce a specially shaped flake, the Middle Stone Age sees more extensive development of such techniques. Smaller cores were worked in a more complex fashion and finer grained rocks were often used. Tools were hafted on to shafts with adhesives made of plant gums tempered with ochre. Experiments by Lyn Wadley and her students show that this was a complex task that required serious attention to the details of working with different types of resins and woods – an early example of multitasking. Such techniques indicate that Middle Stone Age cognitive abilities were more akin to our own, which allow continued learning and the acquisition of new skills over an extended period of adolescent brain development. The archaeological and fossil records of Africa have, indeed, vouchsafed to the world a unique history, spanning more than 2 million years, of milestones in the development of those special features which make us human.

CENTIMETRES

Early hominids at Swartkrans used more chert flakes (above left) than at Sterkfontein because good chert was easily available at the site; but quartz and quartzite were used also (flakes above centre and right). Clear evidence for butchery of animals is present at Swartkrans in the form of bones with cut marks (above centre). Among the early tool-bearing sites in the Cradle (2 to 1 million years old), Swartkrans has the largest proportion of cut-marked bones – the clearest evidence for hominid butchery among all of the Cradle of Humankind sites. The flakes shown here are from C.K. Brain's excavations in the oldest deposit at Swartkrans, the Lower Bank of Member 1, dated by fauna to about 1.7 million years.

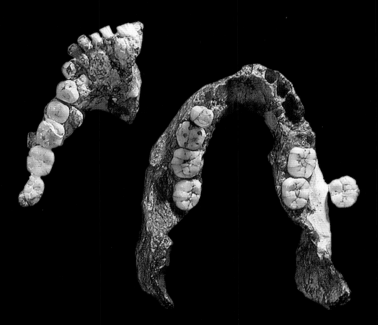

In Swartkrans Member 2, Early Acheulean artefacts are associated with *Homo ergaster* fossils . At Sterkfontein, a crushed partial mandible StW 80 (above left) and other teeth are in direct association with Acheulean tools. The isolated molar is part of StW 80 and is shown with SK 15 from Swartkrans.

Swartkrans contains artefacts and cut-marked bones in all three of the older infills, dating from about 1.7 to 1.0 million years ago. The excavation shown above is in the Lower Bank of Member 1, the oldest deposit, where the artefacts may belong to the Oldowan Industry. The tools in Members 2 and 3 are of Early Acheulean age. The view (above bottom) is from the cave looking upwards towards the open excavation area.

CENTIMETRES

Above left: During renewed excavations at Swartkrans led by Travis Pickering and Morris Sutton, a loose portion of the Member 1 Hanging Remnant was removed by blasting in 2006. Colour coding the deposits to be blasted insured their original positions could be identified in the rubble left by the blast.
Above right: At the nearby Kromdraai A site the deposits are somewhat younger. Recent excavations by Francis Thackeray have yielded more than one hundred stone tools belonging to the Early Acheulean; no cleavers or handaxes have yet been found but this rough pick in quartz belongs to that tradition.

Kromdraai B deposits (above) are about 1. 9 million years old but have yielded only a few certain stone tools. The habitat was locally moist and closed, which mirrors conditions during the Sterkfontein Oldowan infilling. There are also some similarities between a *Paranthropus robustus* tooth found in the Sterkfontein Oldowan and *Paranthropus robustus* at the Kromdraai B site.

CENTIMETRES

CENTIMETRES

Above and opposite page: Large cutting tools of the Early Acheulean include handaxes, cleavers and picks, all of which were made for heavy duty tasks. These examples are from Sterkfontein.

CENTIMETRES

Flakes, blades and retouched flake tools are the hallmark of the Middle Stone Age, replacing the large handaxes and cleavers which are diagnostic of the Acheulean. At Swartkrans, the artefacts (above) are dated to less than 110,000 years ago, which is the date for a flowstone underlying the deposit. At Sterkfontein, Middle Stone Age hominids were present prior to 115,000 years.

The younger deposits at Sterkfontein and Swartkrans attest to the presence of modern *Homo sapiens* in the Cradle of Humankind. At Swartkrans, new excavations by Morris Sutton of Middle Stone Age deposits (above) show that modern humans occupied land on the surface close to one of the cave entrances. Below, researcher Jason Heaton emerges from a chamber where a dated flowstone underlies the Middle Stone Age deposit.

Chapter SIX
DENIZENS OF THE WOODLAND AND SAVANNAH

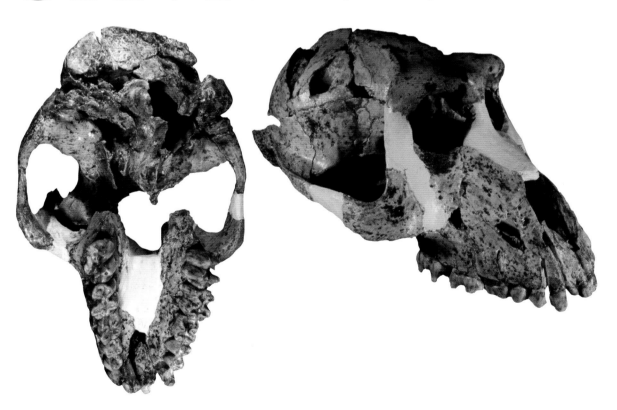

Two views of a female *Theropithecus oswaldi* (SK 561), an extinct gelada baboon cranium from Swartkrans.

There is a variety of carnivores in the breccia deposits, including hyaenas.

Ancient Animals and Vegetation of the Cradle

Our hominid ancestors were but one representative of the fauna of their time, i.e., of the animals and insects that once occupied the area; these creatures were, in turn, reliant to varying extents on the plants which lived in the surrounding landscape. Thus, if we are to know more about the way of life of our ancestors, it is important to have as great an understanding as possible of the wildlife and plants that had a major impact on their lives and which also give us clues about the past environments and climates of the Cradle.

Fossil wood from Member 4 at Sterkfontein (which has yielded more remains of the hominid *Australopithecus africanus* than any other site) has been cut into thin sections and identified under a microscope by Marion Bamford at the Bernard Price Institute for Palaeontology at the University of the Witwatersrand. She found that many of the fossil wood pieces belong to a species of liana, *Dichapetaleum mobuttense*, that now grows in the dense, humid forests and gallery forests of the Democratic Republic of the Congo and Cameroon and no longer occurs in southern Africa. Moreover, lianas require large trees for their support.

This indicates that, at the time of Australopithecus, Sterkfontein was at least in a gallery forest and possibly a refugium of tropical forest. Further corroboration for this conclusion has been provided by the identification of other fossil wood as belonging to Anastrabe, a shrub that now grows in KwaZulu-Natal under moister, warmer conditions than occur today at Sterkfontein.

Furthermore, the fossil fauna from Member 4, which includes many large monkeys, also suggests the presence of forest; however, other fauna indicate the presence of grassland nearby. Elisabeth Vrba, in a study of the bovid (antelope) fauna from Sterkfontein, Swartkrans and Kromdraai, found that there was a strong presence of the woodland species *Makapania broomi* and *hippotragines* in Sterkfontein Member 4, but that grassland species (*Alcelaphines* and *Antilopines*) were also well represented. It is thus clear that areas of grassland were present near to the forested area of the Sterkfontein caves. *Makapania* is an interesting bovid. It seems to be related to the Takin (*Budorcas*), which today inhabits woodland areas of the Himalayan foothills and which, like *Makapania*, has hooves adapted for climbing in rocky terrain. A very strange animal that lived at Sterkfontein during Member 4 times was the chalicothere, a relative of horses and rhinos, that probably used its large front claws for pulling down vegetation as it fed.

By the time of the accumulation of Member 5 at Sterkfontein, around 2 million years ago, the fauna had changed. The forest-loving *Parapapio* monkeys had been replaced by *Papio* baboons which preferred an open habitat. There were also other grassland species in the form of *Equus*, spring hares and ostrich. The advent of open landscape species coincided with the first appearance at Sterkfontein of early stone tools in the form of the Oldowan Industry. It can thus be seen that the presence of, or absence of, certain animals provides an important indication of changing habitat and climate. In short, a drying trend in Africa had reduced the forest cover at Sterkfontein by about 2 million years ago; the landscape had become even more open by about 1.5 million years ago. Microfaunal studies of the bones of small rodents, insectivores, birds, reptiles and amphibians, which were regurgitated in owl pellets within the caves, also provide useful insights about past environments because these small creatures are closely adapted to habitat and vegetation types such as grassland, forest, swamp, and so on.

The occurrence of a variety of carnivores in the breccia deposits, including giant hyaenas, long-legged hunting hyaenas, leopards, lions, false sabre-toothed cats (*Dinofelis*) and sabre-toothed cats (*Megantereon*), illustrates the constant danger from predators which our ancestors faced. Another important finding of faunal analysis is that the presence of certain species of animal in a faunal assemblage can give an indication of the age of a particular deposit when they have counterparts in well dated assemblages in East Africa.

**Top: The extinct chalicothere, a relative of horses and rhinos, which probably used its large front claws for pulling down vegetation as it fed.
Above: Chalicothere middle phalanx of foot from Sterkfontein Member 4.**

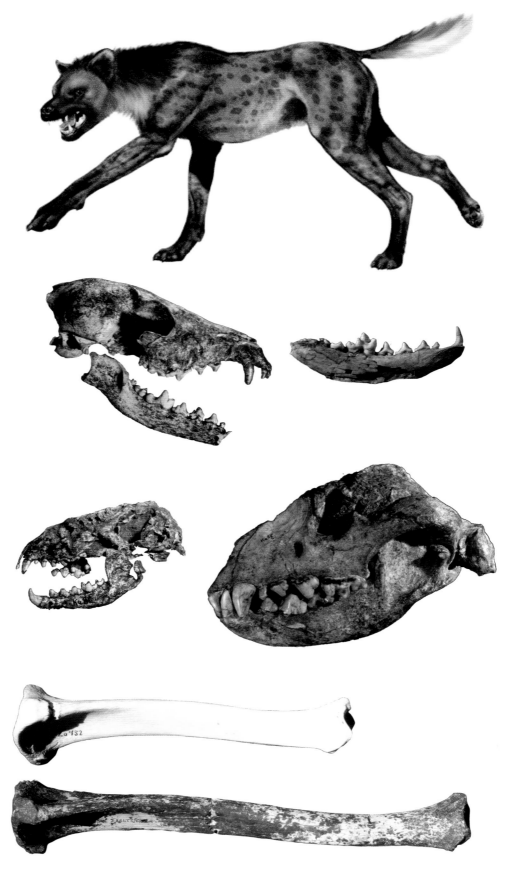

Top: Long-legged hunting hyaena, *Chasmaporthetes*, now extinct, once lived in the Cradle.
Second from top, left : Jackal skull, *Canis mesomelas,* from Kromdraai.
Second from top, right : Lower jaw of a fox, *Vulpes pulcher,* from Kromdraai.
Second from bottom, left: Mongoose skull, *Herpestes mesotes,* from Kromdraai.
Second from bottom, right: Giant hyaena skull, *Pachycrocuta,* from Kromdraai.
Bottom: *Chasmaporthetes* tibia from Sterkfontein compared to the modern hyaena tibia above it.

**Top: How the extinct *Makapania* bovid may have looked.
Above: A fossil horn core of a *Makapania* from Sterkfontein and a
partial skull of *Makapania* from Makapansgat.**

Top: A representation of the *Parapapio* genus of monkeys which inhabited forests.
Above: Fossils of three monkeys of the genus *Parapapio* from Sterkfontein Member 2.

Top: A representation of the colobus monkey that *Australopithecus* would have seen in the forests. Above: Fossil of colobus monkey *(Cercopithecoides williamsi)* from Bolt's Farm near Sterkfontein.

Modern baboon.

Top: Baboon fossil, *Papio angusticeps* female, from Kromdraai.
Centre: Baboon fossil, *Gorgopithecus major* (facial view), from Kromdraai.
Bottom: Baboon fossil, *Gorgopithecus major* (basal view), from Kromdraai.

Top: Representation of the false sabre-toothed cat, *Dinofelis*.
Above: The false sabre-toothed cat, *Dinofelis barlowi*, from Kromdraai.

The teeth are upper canines from Sterkfontein of true sabre-toothed cats.
The one on the right is *Machaerodus* from Bolt's Farm and the two on the left are from
one individual of *Megantereon* from Sterkfontein.

Chapter SEVEN

WHERE TO FROM HERE

Cultural progress: from the Acheulean handaxe to the modern city.

Landcape of the Cradle of Humankind.

The fossil sites of the Cradle of Humankind document 3 million years of interaction between our forebears and the environment of one small area of Planet Earth. The picture which emerges from the bones and their host deposits at around the time of *Austrolopithecus* shows how deep a dependence this hominid had on its natural surroundings.

No evidence has survived to tell us how it may have made use of the natural resources that these provided. In time the environment came to be more systematically exploited as the making and use of stone (and probably also wooden) tools began in the area, around 2 million years ago, with the appearance of the Oldowan Industry.

The earliest Stone-Age populations were certainly sparse and the uneasy co-existence between man and his natural predators (such as hunting hyenas, sabre-toothed cats and lions) was aided little by the early tool kits. In short, the pressure exerted on the natural environment by *Australopithecus*, *Paranthropus* and *Homo* was minimal.

The first significant impacts were probably felt only some time after 1 million years ago with the advent of the controlled use of fire, (recent data from Europe place the date for the earliest use of fire there around 790 000 years ago, but see also Chapter 5). The interior plateau of South Africa has always been subject to periodic bush fires kindled by lightning strikes; any increase in the frequency of burning would have contributed to the shrinking of gallery forests, which was already occurring at that time under the influence of natural climate change.

Acheulean tool, a handaxe, from Sterkfontein.

The environment of Stone Age Africa probably changed little over the ensuing hundreds of millennia. The next – and very much more serious – upswing in environmental pressure coincided with the arrival of Bantu-speaking Iron Age pastoralists from the north in the second or third centuries A.D. These immigrants brought with them cattle, the cultivation of millet and sorghum and the smelting of iron and copper. Opening up of the bush, both to increase grazing resources and to create areas for cultivation, was achieved by slash-and-burn methods. Clearings probably remained small and patchy and although the hunting of game was practised, the scale was small. With the establishment of trade links with Arab, and later Portuguese, colonists along the east coast of Africa, hunting pressures increased to satisfy demands for ivory and skins; small-scale gold and tin mining added to the range of goods available for barter. As populations grew, extensive stone-walled settlements and agricultural terraces were constructed in some areas (the remains of several can be seen in the area between the Cradle and Rustenburg). Competition for resources and the control of trade routes eventually brought internal conflict, which culminated in the Difaqane (civil wars) of the 1820s in which many people were killed or displaced and large areas of agricultural land were abandoned.

At around this time the first waves of Voortrekkers were beginning to arrive in the area – Dutch colonists from the Cape who had migrated ever further north to escape the restrictive rule of the colonial regimes established by Britain as it extended its hegemony over ever increasing tracts of the South African interior in pursuit of its considerable mineral wealth. With the Voortrekkers came western agricultural technology and a variety of skills that led eventually to the establishment of the first towns in proximity of the Cradle: Pretoria and Rustenburg. By 1881 gold had been discovered in the area (Chapter 1); by 1896 the first systematic mining of the gold-bearing reefs of the Witwatersrand had begun.

Voortrekker wagon.

Iron Age stone walls.

The dawn of the 20th Century saw a landscape which, although not completely transformed by human activity, preserved few areas where its imprint was not widely evident. One such area was the Cradle. Throughout the 20th Century this rural enclave, located just beyond the peri-urban fringes of Krugersdorp and Pretoria, remained little affected by agriculture, except along parts of the Bloubank Valley. The discovery and exploration of its astounding fossil sites from the 1930s onward fortunately brought little commercial development, so that, at the time of its proclamation by UNESCO as South Africa's first World Heritage Site in 1999, its rural and largely unspoilt character remained intact. Its proclamation under the custodianship of the Gauteng Provincial Government has ensured that the Cradle's natural assets and fossil treasury will continue to be preserved for the benefit of all of humanity.

Where to Now?

The first decade of the 21st Century, will surely be remembered for the widespread acceptance, both by governments and common citizens, of the perils which threaten our planet as a result of human abuse of its environment. One of the most important international responses was the establishment, two decades ago, of the International Geosphere-Biosphere Programme (IGBP).

A major part of the brief of the IGBP is to further our understanding of present and future climate change, through an analysis of the nature, causes and mechanisms of changes that occurred in the past and are continuing to occur now. These changes are recorded by natural archives such as deep-sea sediments, tree rings, cores from glaciers and the polar ice-caps, and lake sediments. There was much debate among scientists within the IGBP, during the first decade of its existence, on how to make both governments and the public aware of climate change as a phenomenon; most importantly, the IGBP strove to highlight the role of human activities, especially the continued emission of "greenhouse" gases such as carbon dioxide, methane and nitrous oxide in changing the natural environment, perhaps irrevocably. There is now widespread consensus that the quantity of greenhouse gases in the atmosphere has increased dramatically since the start of the Industrial Revolution to a level double that of pre-industrial times (see figure on opposite page). Greenhouse gasses allow short-wavelength radiation from the sun to pass through them to warm the surface of the earth;

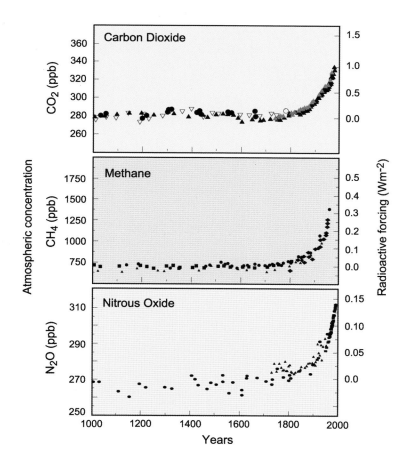

Changes in concentrations of the most common greenhouse gases in the Earth's atmosphere over the last 1000 years (compiled from a variety of sources).

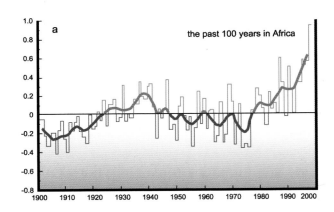

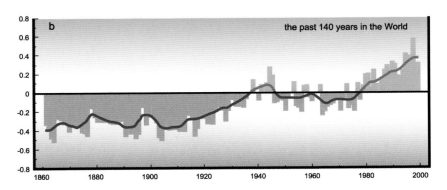

Variations of the Earth's surface temperature for a) the past 100 years in Africa and b) the past 140 years in the world. (Source: World Meteorological Organisation).

this warmth is re-radiated into the atmosphere in longer wavebands. Most of this outgoing radiation cannot pass through the atmosphere and is trapped by it, causing the atmosphere to heat up (see diagram above). In simple terms this is the mechanism which drives global warming.

Teams of scientists working across the globe have now assembled an unambiguous body of evidence for the reality of this phenomenon. The diagram overleaf summarises the natural temperature changes that have occurred since the Last Glacial Period, some 20 000 years ago, when the average global temperature was about 5 degrees centigrade lower than today. Landmark events are highlighted and the projected extent of future global warming due to human influences is added at the end of the curve. It is clear that temperatures are now higher than they have been over the last 20 000 years, and records from ice cores recovered from Antarctica confirm that they are, indeed, higher than at any time during the last 400 000 years.

African sunset.

Above: Alternate form of energy; a windmill power plant.
Photograph courtesy of Jesper Baerentzen.

In recent years the willingness of most governments to place global warming on their agendas, and of some to introduce measures to reduce emissions of greenhouse gases, has been an important advance, but many scientists consider that these responses amount to 'too little too late'. Concentrations of greenhouse gases in the atmosphere continue to rise while 'alternative technologies', using renewable resources to provide energy (e.g. solar panels and wind turbines), have proved slow to perfect; furthermore the energy which they produce is difficult to use conveniently and efficiently in powering cars, which emit a significant proportion of the present world output of greenhouse gases. Reliance on non-renewable energy sources (fossil fuels such as coal, oil and gas) and, perhaps, the increased use of nuclear power (with associated waste disposal issues) are therefore likely to continue in the short to medium term.

How will this affect the future of a species whose lineage has inhabited this planet for more than 5 million years? Some of the damage already caused by global warming is probably irreversible, given that the volumes of greenhouse gases in the atmosphere will continue to rise (but probably more slowly) as emission controls and renewable energy substitutes are phased in, after which – if all goes to plan – they could possibly stabilise, but will certainly not reduce.

One such irreversible impact is the loss of very large volumes of the earth's surface ice through the melting of glaciers as well as both of the earth's polar ice-caps: the arctic ice-cap has shrunk in area by 8.1% in the past 30 years (see diagram overleaf) and, according to NASA, has (more frighteningly) thinned by as much as 40% in the past 5 years. Sea level has been increasing in concert with this melting: a rise of 18cm has occurred over the last century and some estimates suggest that, even with reduced greenhouse emissions, it may increase by a further 50cm by 2050. The threat to low lying and heavily populated areas such as the coast of Bangladesh is obvious.

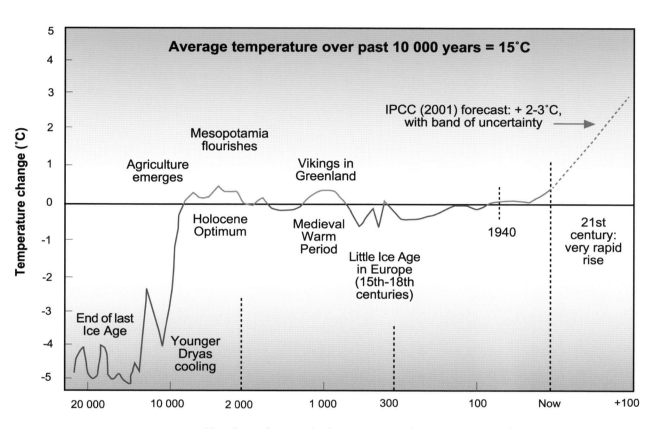

**Variations in the earth's average surface temperature over the past 20 000 years.
(Source: McMichael et al, WHO, 2003)**

Melting ice-caps.
Photograph courtesy of Ariel da Silva Parreira.

Ice loss and sea-level rise are serious but not, on their own, threats to our future survival. Much more significant will be the impacts on food production and fresh water resources which changes in the circulation of the atmosphere and oceans are already starting to bring. Present atmospheric circulations are driven by temperature contrasts; these contrasts are inherent in the natural temperature gradient from equator to poles, the distribution of the continental land masses in relation to the oceans, differences in surface elevation of the land, differences in reflectivity of the surface (e.g. ice as opposed to water, rock or dense vegetation), as well as a number of other factors.

With global warming the pattern and amplitude of temperature contrasts across the globe will change; this is already occurring as a result of melting of the polar ice. As circulations undergo increasing modification climatic belts will shift, sometimes dramatically. Areas that are now humid will dry out, and vice versa; ocean current-systems such as the Gulf Stream, which moderates climates in Western Europe and eastern North America through its transfer of warm water to high latitudes, may change position or even cease to operate; this holds potentially catastrophic consequences for huge populations in the continental areas around the margins of the North Atlantic ocean. Another possible consequence of potential global significance is the melting of the permafrost (permanently frozen soil) in the northern tundra areas of Canada and Russia; this could release millions of cubic metres of methane from the underlying peat deposits, which would significantly raise the overall level of this greenhouse gas in the atmosphere.

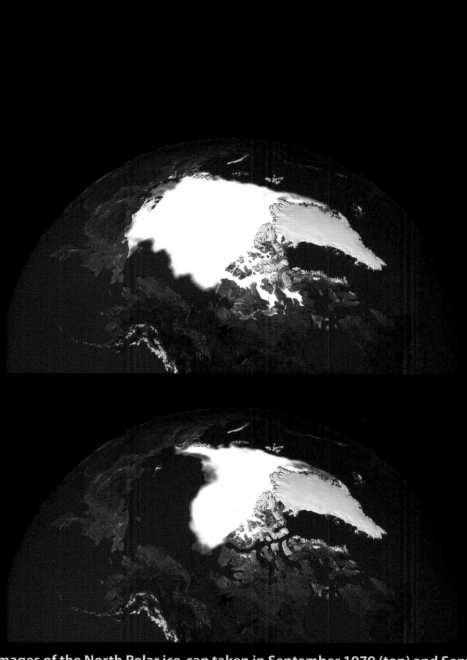

Satellite images of the North Polar ice-cap taken in September 1979 (top) and September 2007 (below) showing significant loss of ice area within the 28 year period. (Source: NASA)

Power plant pollution.

Most climatic modellers consider it likely, also, that the frequency and intensity of individual climatic events is likely to increase as the atmosphere warms. More frequent and severe droughts, bigger floods and more severe hurricanes are likely to result. The list of unwelcome consequences is, in fact, well-nigh inexhaustible; what they have in common is their adverse impact on food and water resources that are already under pressure across the globe. The diagram on the opposite page shows just how seriously increasing drought is likely to affect soil moisture availability in South Africa, upon which the food security of our entire population, now approaching 50 million people, is critically dependent. Yet, as the early ape-men have shown us, the hominids have an extraordinary capacity for survival. Many of the natural climate changes and extreme events which occurred during the millions of years over which our ancestors occupied this planet must have been similarly devastating, especially to those lacking the ability to protect themselves adequately from the elements.

But, in the final analysis, our options may be as limited as those of the most vulnerable of the ape-men: adapt or perish. Unless we, as a species, can come to appreciate the consequences of our actions, unless we can learn to become responsible custodians of our environment, the risk of extinction looms large. The fossil record documents a number of global extinction events through which a few species only survived to re-colonise a near-lifeless planet. The Cradle of Humankind itself provides evidence of one such extinction during the time of our own early ancestors: Paranthropus, whose remains are the most abundant of any hominid found in the Cradle, disappeared completely from the fossil record shortly before one million years ago. Does modern humanity, with its armamentarium of technical aids and computer resources, possess the insight to curb its own greed sufficiently to pre-empt a similar fate?

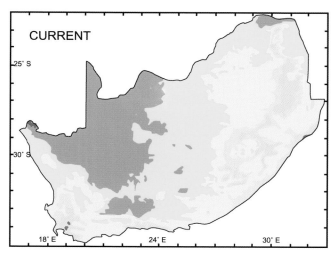

Soil moisture days measured in 1990 (360 ppm CO_2)

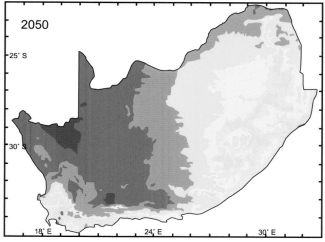

Soil moisture days predicted for 2050 (550 ppm CO_{20})

The number of days of favourable soil moisture measured in South Africa in 1990 (atmospheric CO_2 content 360 ppm) (above) compared with estimated favourable soil moisture days in 2050 (projected atmospheric CO_2 content 550ppm) (below). Source: B Hewitson 1999.

Without trees our world would be a physical and cultural desert.

In Chapter 1 of this book mention was made of the long-dominant power of religion in suppressing attempts by enlightened human beings to understand where we come from and how we relate to our environment. These attempts to suppress knowledge unfortunately continue in many areas today. Mankind would be better served if the religious fundamentalists paid attention to the statement in Genesis 3 Verse 19 'for dust thou art, and unto dust shalt thou return.' Yes, we are all composed of cosmic dust – planet earth, plants, and animals including humans - and thus we are all inter-linked.

In the natural order, when humans and animals die their bodies and bones decay and become dust of the ground. That dust provides nutrients for plants that will, in turn, provide new sustenance for animals and humans. This is the cycle of life through which humans, animals and plants depend upon one another. The hunter-gatherer peoples of the world are aware of this and know, not only how to utilise their environment, but also the importance of preserving it.

Ironically, it is human cultural success in the form of urbanisation and advanced technology that has divorced humans from their roots and led to disregard and disrespect for the environment. Food is purchased in elaborate packaging in supermarkets and transported home in motor vehicles produced and powered using finite resources, wood is obtained ready-cut in timber yards without thought of the distant forests that produced it, water is readily available at the turn of a tap and light from the flick of a switch. If we are to endure as a species then urban people must, like their hunter-gatherer cousins, be educated from childhood to appreciate and preserve their environment.

Contemporary landscape at the Cradle of Humankind.

"All indications are that our early ancestry was in the forests and that trees provided our ancestors with food sources and a safe refuge during the day – but especially at night. The types of forest that nurtured our ancestors provide for us still today and also provide homes for a host of wildlife. We benefit from food resources and from the medicines that derive from trees, and for centuries we have used wood to construct houses, ships and furniture. Without trees our world would be a physical and cultural desert and thus it is in the best interests of all human beings to value and protect the forests that are left. What is the use of being religiously devout in the hope of an afterlife when we cannot look after the world and this life that was provided for us?

Thus the allegory of Adam and Eve has a special meaning. The eating of the fruit of the tree of knowledge of good and evil supposedly set humans apart from the animals. Humans alone know right from wrong and, to put it simply, it is right to create and wrong to destroy, whether it be destruction of life and well-being, property, or environment. Throughout the long process of evolution of human beings, our brains have so developed that by the mid 18th century Linnaeus classified humans as Homo sapiens. Humankind's accumulated and ever-expanding wisdom concerning the world we live in, and the universe beyond our world, is extraordinary. Yet this wisdom has been and still is marred by destructive actions which are the very antithesis of wisdom and are indicative of a perverted use of human knowledge for the personal gain or power of a few. Such actions include warfare in pursuit of dominance or greed for territory and material wealth, mental and physical cruelty usually in the name of political or religious dogma, destruction of wildlife and forests, and pollution of air and water and landscape. Something is radically wrong with the so-called wise man, and if religions are to play a meaningful and positive role, they should eschew all harmful dogma from the inadequately enlightened past and rather help to eradicate destructive behaviour and promote the evolution of wisdom."
– Ronald J. Clarke

From a chapter in *When Worlds Converge – What Science and Religion Tell Us about the Story of the Universe and our Place in it.* (Open Court Publishers, Chicago 2002.)

Chapter EIGHT

WHERE TO VISIT AND WHAT TO SEE

Signifiers at the entrance to Maropeng.

The Tumulus building at Maropeng.

Maropeng Visitor's Centre

Just a few kilometers away from Johannesburg and Pretoria is the area now known as the Cradle of Humankind. It is a vast mass of bush and grassland which shows a part of Africa as it was millions of years ago. This stark, sometimes barren land is where many caves were discovered and today, driving through 47,000 hectares of the first World Heritage Site in Africa, you will come across the Cradle of Humankind and sites of the earliest discoveries of such famous scientists as Robert Broom, Bob Brain and Ron Clarke in the Sterkfontein and Swartkrans Caves.

It is an amazing experience to discover the many options of hotels, restaurants and interesting places to visit in the Cradle, some of which equal any to be found in other heritage sites in the world. We have selected two establishments in different parts of the Cradle to 'whet your appetite' but there are other options listed here in this chapter to suit your taste.

Exhibition at Maropeng Visitor Centre.

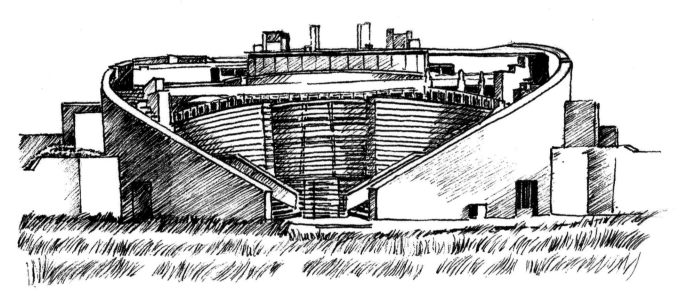

The Maropeng Visitor Centre at the Cradle of Humankind.

A suggestion for a first visit would be to take a weekend break through the Crocodile Ramble from Honeydew westwards, which will lead you to the heart of the Cradle of Humankind and to the Maropeng Visitor's Centre which is built on the edge of the Cradle World Heritage Site. It is the official visitor centre and a site where hundreds of stone tools were discovered.

On entering the spectacular architectural structure of the Maropeng Museum via a craft market you will reach the Tumulus building which is reminiscent of an ancient burial mound, with a timeline of Earth's history, leading to an underwater boat ride. The ride will take you back in time through the elements of water, air, earth and fire. Passing through a vortex, you will be transported back into the distant past to when the super-continent of Gondwanaland slowly drifted apart over millions of years to form the continents as we know them today. As you emerge you will witness the origins of life, the changing environment and the looming threat of what scientists are predicting may be the sixth mass extinction in the history of the planet.

Above and opposite page: Exhibition displays at the Maropeng Visitor Centre at the Cradle of Humankind.

The Sterkfontein Caves Visitor Centre.

Sterkfontein Caves

Ten minutes away can be found the Sterkfontein Museum which is both spectacular and fascinating. Opposite is Swartkrans, a site some scientists believe to have evidence of some of the oldest human control of fire dating back to over 1 million years ago. Another 8 kilometres away visit the Rhino and Lion Nature Reserve and Wonder Cave (formerly Van Wyk's Pothole) comprising a vast 2.2 million-year-old chamber with well preserved stalactites, stalagmites, columns and a variety of fascinating and beautiful dripstone formations. The cave has an example of a relatively young talus cone. Take a safari break and discover the animal and bird life in the reserve, after which you can enjoy a local braai (barbecue) at the Ngomo VIP Camp, and taste the local sausage (wors) made with game, along with local maize meal porridge (pap).

A visit to the unique Lesedi Cultural Village is worthwhile to absorb the old traditions of Africa. Its display of traditional African tribal folklore showcases different tribal homesteads of the Ndebele, Zulu, Basotho, Xhosa and Pedi. Watch the traditional dancing and visit a witch doctor (sangoma), who will throw bones to tell your fortune, after which you can experience a true African feast.

Day tours are available through a number of tour companies operating from either Johannesburg or Pretoria. For more information contact the Crocodile Ramble at www.theramble.co.za

Displays in the Sterkfontein Caves Visitor Centre.

Glossary

Acheulean	A long-lived Earlier Stone Age industry characterised by handaxes and cleavers, originating in Africa about 1.7 million years ago, which spread into Europe, the Middle East and parts of Asia, until it was replaced by the Middle Stone Age
Alluvial	Created or deposited by river action
Bantu	A family of languages belonging to Negroid peoples who migrated into southern Africa from the north
Bipedal	Walking on two legs, a defining feature of hominids
Breccia (or cave breccia)	The sediment and broken rock infilling of a cave that has become cemented into a hard deposit by calcium carbonate
Chert	A hard sedimentary rock consisting of silicon dioxide
Cleaver	A large stone tool typical of Acheulean industries, characterised by a sharp cutting end or edge and an axe-like shape
Cognitive	With the capacity to acquire knowledge and to reason
Conduit	A channel through which material (e.g., sediment and water) can pass
Continuum	A continuous series of objects or events
Cosmogenic Nuclide	An unstable form of an element produced by cosmic ray activity in the atmosphere which is subject to radioactive decay into other forms
Diabase	A basic rock formed by the solidification of molten material from the earth's interior
Dripstone	A hard deposit, usually of calcium carbonate, formed by precipitation of carbonate from water dripping within a cave
Fissure	A long, narrow cleft in rock
Flowstone	A hard deposit, usually of calcium carbonate, formed by precipitation of carbonate from water flowing within a cave
Genus	A group into which a family of animals or plants is divided and which contains one or more species
Handaxe	A large flaked stone tool typical of Acheulean industries, characterised by a pointed working end and often by sharp cutting edges
Hegemony	Leadership or dominance
Hominid	A bipedal primate classed within the zoological family Hominidae, which includes *Australopithecus*, *Paranthropus* and *Homo*, as well as earlier forms (*Sahelanthropus*, *Orrorin*, and *Ardipithecus*)
Homo neanderthalensis	A heavy-browed form of *Homo* (the human genus) which lived in Europe at the same time as *Homo sapiens* but became extinct about 27 000 years ago
Isotope	A form of a particular element with a different atomic weight from other forms; some isotopes are unstable and decay into other forms or elements and can be used for dating purposes
Lemur	A general name for the more than 35 species of lower primates that live only in Madagascar
Loris	A general name for small, nocturnal lower primates, comprising the lorises of India, Sri Lanka and southeast Asia, and the potto, angwantibo and bushbabies (*Galago*) of Africa
Mandible	Lower jaw
Manuport	A stone not naturally occurring in a site but carried in by hominids
Mass spectrometer	A laboratory instrument for determining, with great precision, the isotopic constituents of a rock or bone sample
Maxilla	Upper jaw

Methane	A gas, sometimes known as marsh gas, which is produced by the decomposition of vegetable matter under water or the burning of fuels; an important "greenhouse" gas
Middle Stone Age	A complex of stone tool industries from about 300,000 to 30,000 years ago, characterised by smaller formal tools than in the Acheulean, including pointed flake tools; flakes (and sometimes blades) can be produced with advanced methods of core preparation
Miocene	A period of geological time lasting from 23.5 to 5.3 million years ago
Neogene	A broad subdivision of geological time which includes the Miocene and the Pliocene and spans the period 23.5 to 2.6 million years ago (or to 1.8 million years ago by older definitions)
Nitrous oxide	An oxide of nitrogen produced by the burning of fuels; an important "greenhouse" gas
Oldowan	The earliest stone tool industries dating from almost 2.6 to 1.7 million years ago in Africa, characterised by simple cores and flakes, and preceding the Acheulean
Palaeomagnetism	The magnetism acquired in the past by a rock or sediment sample from the then prevailing magnetic field of the earth; under certain circumstances it may be compared to the present magnetic field as an aid to dating
Perennial	Occurring or continuing throughout the year
Pleistocene	A period of geological time extending from 2.6 million years (or in earlier definitions, 1.8 million years) to about 10 000 years ago
Pliocene	A period of geological time extending from 5.3 to 2.6 million years ago (or 1.8 million years in earlier definitions)
Premaxilla	The small bone in which the incisor teeth are rooted at the front of the upper jaw
Primate	A member of the zoological group of mammals that includes lemurs, lorises, tarsiers, monkeys, apes and hominids
Promulgate	To proclaim a law or regulation
Quaternary	A broad division of geological time encompassing the Pleistocene and the Holocene and thus spanning the period 2.6 million years (or 1.8 million years in earlier definitions) to the present
Savannah	A vegetation cover consisting of grass with a scattering of trees
Stalactite	A formation, usually of calcium carbonate, which hangs from a cave roof and is formed by precipitation of the carbonate out of dripping water
Stalagmite	A formation, usually of calcium carbonate, which grows upwards from the floor of a cave, often as a result of precipitation of carbonate from water dripping from a stalactite above it
Stratigraphy	The sequence of layers deposited as sediments or rocks accumulated through time
Talus cone	A conical mound of debris which forms beneath an opening in a cave roof through which sediment and rubble fall
Taphonomy	The study of what happens to a body between death and burial, including the damage occurring on bones with a view to determining the agents of accumulation and modification of bone
Tarsier	A small nocturnal primate, found in the Philippines, Borneo, Sumatra and Sulawesi, which has very large eyes and powerful hind legs for leaping
Tertiary	A broad period of geological time, the use of which has been largely abandoned; it spans the period 65 million years to 2.6 million years ago (or 1.8 million years in earlier definitions)
Travertine	A chemical precipitate of carbonate material which usually accumulates around a spring; sometimes used loosely to include speleothem deposits (the carbonate formations that occur in caves)
Tundra	Vast treeless plains of the high latitudes of North America and Europe with an Arctic climate and vegetation and containing extensive peat deposits

Acknowledgements

The authors are deeply grateful to Kathleen Kuman for taking responsibility for Chapter 5 and for her important contributions to the book as a whole and to Jason Heaton for his meticulous photography and Photoshop editing of many hominid photos. Reshma Lakha-Singh of the Cradle of Humankind World Heritage Site and Dinokeng Blue IQ Projects, administered by the Gauteng Provincial Government, gave support throughout the gestation of this volume and provided detailed contact information on accommodation venues within the Cradle. This book grew out of an idea conceived by Susie Jordan Partridge, whose enthusiasm, encouragement and coercion have contributed in no small measure to its realisation. We thank the Ditsong National Natural History Museum (formerly the Transvaal Museum, Pretoria) and Stephany Potze for permission to photograph fossils and artefacts in their care. Excavation and research at Sterkfontein was initiated by Prof. P.V. Tobias with Alun Hughes and has been supported by: the University of the Witwatersrand, the Palaeontological Scientific Trust, the Ford Foundation, the Mott Foundation, the Embassy of France in South Africa, the National Research Foundation, the De Beers Chairman's Fund, the National Geographic Society, the Wenner Gren Foundation, and the L.S.B Leakey Foundation.

We would like to acknowledge the following people and institutions for information, photographs and images used in this book:

Front cover: Little Foot photograph by R.J. Clarke; Taung Child photograph by Heaton and Clarke, courtesy of the School of Anatomical Sciences, University of the Witwatersrand
Back cover: Top photograph by R.J. Clarke, courtesy of the Ditsong National Natural History Museum; middle and bottom photographs by Heaton and Clarke, courtesy of the Ditsong National Natural History Museum; photograph of Ron Clarke by Stephen Motsumi
Title page: Illustration by Janet Berger

Page 3: Illustration by Janet Berger

Page 4: Illustration by Janet Berger

Page 5: Photograph by C.K. Brain

Page 6: Illustration by Janet Berger

Page 7: Left and centre photographs courtesy of Maropeng/Flow Communications, photograph on right by R.J. Clarke

Introduction

Page 8: Photograph by Tim Partridge

Page 9: Three photographs courtesy of Maropeng/Flow Communications

Page11: The Taung Child reconstruction by Robert Broom (1950): *Finding the Missing Link*. London: Watts and Co.

Page 12: Left photograph courtesy of the Martinaglia family; right photograph by R.J. Clarke

Page 14: Two photographs courtesy of Maropeng/Flow Communications

Page 15: Diagrams drawn by Wendy Voorvelt from originals by R.J. Clarke

Chapter 1

Page 18: Photograph by Heaton and Clarke, courtesy of the School of Anatomical Sciences, University of the Witwatersrand

Page 19: Original image photographed from an 18th Century print by Hulk, published in Buffon's *Histoire Naturelle, Générale et Particuliére*

Page 20: Top left photograph by Steve Bloom, 1999, in *Affen, Eine Hommage*. Published in Germany: Verlagsgesellschaft: Konemann Verlagsgesellschaf.; top right photograph by Michael Leach, 1996, in *The Great Apes, Our Face in Nature's Mirror*. Published in London by Blandford; bottom print circa 1575 by Sebastian Munster, published in *Cosmographen*

Page 21: Print circa 1575 by Sebastian Munster, published in *Cosmographen*

Page 22: Photograph of Lord Monboddo from an old print; photograph of Darwin attributed to Julia Margaret Cameron, 1869, although it has been suggested that this is a reversed image of a photograph taken by Leonard Darwin in the 1870s

Page 23: Photograph of Thomas Henry Huxley, with sketch of gorilla skull, date c1870.

Page 24: Illustration by Gabriel Max, courtesy of Senckenberg Museum, Frankfurt, Germany

Page 25: Drawing by A. Forestier, published in *The World We Live In*, edited by Graeme Williams, London, The Waverley Book Company Ltd, 1915

Page 26: Top photograph of Raymond Dart, courtesy of Barlow Rand; bottom photograph from archives of the School of Anatomical Sciences, University of the Witwatersrand

Page 27: Photograph by Heaton and Clarke, courtesy of the School of Anatomical Sciences, University of the Witwatersrand

Page 28: Photograph by Heaton and Clarke, courtesy of the School of Anatomical Sciences, University of the Witwatersrand

Page 29: Top photograph courtesy of the Ditsong National Natural History Museum; bottom drawing by Robert Broom (1950): *Finding the Missing Link*. London: Watts and Co.

Page 31: Photograph by Heaton and Clarke, courtesy of the School of Anatomical Sciences, University of the Witwatersrand

Page 32: Photograph by R.J. Clarke

Page 33: Photograph by Heaton and Clarke

Chapter 2

Page 34: Photographs by Heaton and Clarke, courtesy of the Ditsong National Natural History Museum

Page 35: Left photograph by Carlo Kaminsky; right photograph by R.J. Clarke

Page 36: Illusration after a reconstruction by Tim Partridge

Page 37: Photographs on left by Tim Partridge; right photograph by R.J. Clarke

Page 38: Photograph courtesy of Maropeng/Flow Communications

Page 39: Drawing by Tim Partridge

Page 40: Illustration by Janet Berger

Page 41: Top photograph by K. Kuman; bottom photograph courtesy of Maropeng/Flow Communications

Page 42: Illustration by Janet Berger

Page 43: Photographs by Tim Partridge

Page 44: Record from Lisiecki, L. E., and M. E. Raymo (2005), A Pliocene-Pleistocene stack of 57 globally distributed benthic $\delta^{18}O$ records, *Paleoceanography,* 20, PA1003

Page 45: Graphics after reconstructions by C.K. Brain, with permission

Page 46: Reconstruction after R.J. Clarke (2006): A deeper understanding of the stratigraphy of Sterkfontein fossil hominid site. *Transactions of the Royal Society of South Africa* 66: 111-120.

Page 47: Photograph by K. Kuman

Page 48: Illustration by Janet Berger; research referred to by Jan Kramers, Robyn Pickering, Jo Walker and Bob Cliff.

Page 49: Top photograph courtesy of the Cradle of Humankind; bottom photograph by Carlo Kaminsky

Page 50: Photographs courtesy of Maropeng/Flow Communications, research referred to by Darryl Granger and colleagues. Age range Robyn Pickering

Page 51: Photograph by Tim Partridge

Chapter 3

Page 52: Photographs by Heaton and Clarke, courtesy of the Ditsong National Natural History Museum (left), and the School of Anatomical Sciences, University of the Witwatersrand (right)

Page 53: Drawing by R.J. Clarke

Page 54: Top drawing by Robert Broom (1946): *The South African Fossil Ape-Men, the Australopithecinae.* Transvaal Museum Memoir No.2; bottom photographs by Heaton and Clarke, courtesy of the Ditsong National Natural History Museum

Page 55: Top photographs by R.J. Clarke, courtesy of the Ditsong National Natural History Museum; bottom photograph by Heaton and Clarke, courtesy of the Ditsong National Natural History Museum (left), and the School of Anatomical Sciences, University of the Witwatersrand (right)

Page 56: Left and centre photographs by Heaton and Clarke and right photograph by R.J. Clarke, courtesy of the Ditsong National Natural History Museum

Page 57: Top photograph by R.J. Clarke, courtesy of the School of Anatomical Sciences, University of the Witwatersrand; bottom photograph by Heaton and Clarke, courtesy of the Ditsong National Natural History Museum

Page 58: Photographs by Heaton and Clarke, courtesy of the School of Anatomical Sciences, University of the Witwatersrand

Page 59: Photograph by Heaton and Clarke, courtesy of the Ditsong National Natural History Museum

Page 60: Photographs by Heaton and Clarke, courtesy of the Ditsong National Natural History Museum (middle), and the School of Anatomical Sciences, University of the Witwatersrand (top and bottom)

Page 61: Drawing by R.J. Clarke

Page 62: Photographs by R.J. Clarke

Page 63: Photograph of Alun Hughes and Phillip Tobias, from archives of the Palaeoanthropology Research Unit, University of the Witwatersrand

Page 64: Top drawing by R.J. Clarke; bottom photograph by R.J. Clarke

Page 65: Photograph by K. Kuman

Page 66: Drawings by R.J. Clarke

Page 67: Photographs by Heaton and Clarke: top courtesy of the School of Anatomical Sciences; bottom courtesy of the Ditsong National Natural History Museum

Chapter 4

Page 68: Photograph by Heaton and Clarke, courtesy of the Ditsong National Natural History Museum

Page 69: Illustration by Janet Berger

Page 70: Left photograph by Heaton and Clarke, courtesy of the Ditsong National Natural History Museum; right drawing by Robert Broom (1950): *Finding the Missing Link*. London: Watts and Co.

Page 71: Photographs by Heaton and Clarke, courtesy of the Ditsong National Natural History Museum

Page 72: Top photographs by Heaton and Clarke, courtesy of the Ditsong National Natural History Museum; bottom illustration courtesy of C.K. Brain (1976): *The Hunters or the Hunted?* Chicago and London: University of Chicago Press

Page 74: Photographs by Heaton and Clarke, courtesy of the Ditsong National Natural History Museum

Page 75: Photographs by Heaton and Clarke, courtesy of the Ditsong National Natural History Museum

Page 76: Photograph by Heaton and Clarke, courtesy of the Ditsong National Natural History Museum

Page 77: Photograph by Heaton and Clarke, courtesy of the Ditsong National Natural History Museum

Page 78: Photographs by Heaton and Clarke, courtesy of the Ditsong National Natural History Museum

Page 79: Photographs by Heaton and Clarke, courtesy of the Ditsong National Natural History Museum

Chapter 5

Page 80: Photographs by K. Kuman

Page 81: Drawing by R.J. Clarke; new dates for the Sterkfontein Oldowan: personal communication from Darryl Granger and Ryan Gibbon (in preparation for publication)

Page 82: Photographs by K. Kuman

Page 83: Photographs by K. Kuman

Page 84: Photographs by K. Kuman; Oldowan faunal analysis and deathtrap interpretation by Travis R. Pickering (1999): *Taphonomic Interpretations of the Sterkfontein Early Hominid Site (Gauteng, South Africa) Reconsidered in Light of Recent Evidence*. PhD Dissertation, University of Wisconsin at Madison.

Page 85: Photographs by R.J. Clarke

Page 86: Photographs by R.J. Clarke

Page 87: Photographs and drawing by R.J. Clarke

Page 88: Photograph by K. Kuman

Page 89: Left photograph by K. Kuman; right photograph by R.J. Clarke

Page 90: Photograph by K. Kuman of artefact curated at the Ditsong National Natural History Museum

Page 91: Photographs by K. Kuman of artefacts curated at the Ditsong National Natural History Museum

Page 92: Photograph by Morris Sutton

Page 93: Photographs by K. Kuman and R.J. Clarke

Page 94: Photograph by K. Kuman

Page 95: Photographs by Jason Heaton and R.J. Clarke, courtesy of Ditsong National Natural History Museum

Page 96: Photographs by Megan Hanson

Page 97: Photographs by R.J. Clarke

Page 98: Top photograph by K. Kuman; bottom photograph by Jason Heaton

Page 99: Photographs by R.J. Clarke

Page 100: Photographs by K. Kuman

Page 101: Top left photograph by Morris Sutton; top right photograph by K. Kuman, courtesy of the Ditsong National Natural History Museum; bottom photographs by K. Kuman

Page 102: Photographs by K. Kuman

Page 103: Photographs by K. Kuman

Page 104: Photographs courtesy of Morris Sutton

Page 105: Top photograph by K. Kuman; bottom photograph by Christina Rose

Chapter 6

Page 106: Photographs by Heaton and Clarke, courtesy of the Ditsong National Natural History Museum

Page 107: Illustration by Janet Berger

Page 109: Painting (top) courtesy of Maropeng; bottom photograph by R.J. Clarke

Page 110: Painting (top) courtesy of Maropeng; carnivore skull photographs by Heaton and Clarke, courtesy of the Ditsong National Natural History Museum; long bone photographs (bottom) by R.J. Clarke

Page 111: Painting (top) courtesy of Maropeng based on a sketch by R.J. Clarke; bottom photographs by Heaton and Clarke

Page 112: Painting (top) courtesy of Maropeng; bottom photographs by Heaton and Clarke, courtesy of the School of Anatomical Sciences

Page 113: Painting (top) courtesy of Maropeng; bottom photograph by Heaton and Clarke, courtesy of the School of Anatomical Sciences

Page 114: Illustration by Janet Berger

Page 115: Photographs by Heaton and Clarke, courtesy of the Ditsong National Natural History Museum

Page 116: Painting (top) courtesy of Maropeng; bottom photograph by Heaton and Clarke, courtesy of the Ditsong National Natural History Museum

Page 117: Photographs by Heaton and Clarke, courtesy of the Ditsong National Natural History Museum

Chapter 7

Page 118: Photograph by Jason Heaton

Page 119: Photograph courtesy of Maropeng/Flow Communications

Page 120: Photograph by K. Kuman

Page 121: Illustration by Janet Berger

Page 122: Photograph by Amanda Esterhuysen, courtesy of the Archaeology Department, University of the Witwatersrand

Page 123: Charts by Tim Partridge, compiled from a variety of sources

Page 124: Charts sourced from the World Meteorological Organisation

Page 125: Photograph by Flow Communications

Page 126: Photograph courtesy of Jesper Baerentzen

Page 127: Chart sourced in the following publication: McMichael AJ et al. *Climate change and human health: risks and responses.* Geneva, World Health Organisation, 2003

Page 128: Photograph courtesy of Ariel da Silva Parreira

Page 129: Satellite images of the North Polar ice-cap taken in September 1979 (top) and September 2007 (below) showing significant loss of ice area within the 28 year period. Original source: NASA

Page 130: Photograph courtesy of Cheryl Empey

Page 131: The number of days of favourable soil moisture measured in South Africa in 1990: Source: B Hewitson, 1999

Page 132: Photograph by Tim Partridge

Page 133: Photograph courtesy of Flow Communications

Chapter 8

Page 134: Photograph courtesy of Maropeng

Page 135: Photograph courtesy of Maropeng

Page 136: Photographs courtesy of Maropeng/Flow Communications

Page 137: Illustration by Janet Berger

Page 138: Photographs courtesy of Maropeng/Flow Communications

Page 139: Photographs courtesy of Maropeng/Flow Communications

Page 140: Photographs courtesy of Maropeng/Flow Communications

Page 141: Photographs courtesy of Maropeng/Flow Communications

Page 142: Photographs courtesy of Amanzingwe Lodge Conference Centre

Page 143: Photographs courtesy of Amanzingwe Lodge Conference Centre

Page 144: Photographs courtesy of Misty Hills

Page 145: Photographs courtesy of Misty Hills

Acknowledgements

Page 148: Illustration by Janet Berger

Page 153: Illustration by Janet Berger

Page 154: Map by Tim Partridge

MAP OF SELECTED VENUES IN THE CRADLE

Venue	* Rating	Telephone	Mobile	Web Address
1. Aloe Ridge Hotel and Game Reserve	3	011 957 2070	083 263 8264	www.aloeridgehotel.com
2. Ama Cradle Country Lodge	3	011 952 2977	082 828 1344	www.ama-cradle.co.za
3. Amanzingwe Bush Lodge	4	012 205 1108	083 450 6794	www.amanzingwe.co.za
4. Auberge Maroc	3	011-9572748	082-9007999	www.aubergemaroc.co.za
5. Avianto Hotel and Conference Centre	5	011 668 3000		www.avianto.co.za
6. Bergvallei Wedding & Conf. Venue	3	011 662 1172	082 453 8848	www.bergvallei.co.za
7. Budmarsh Private Lodge	5	011 728 1800		www.budmarsh.co.za
8. Carnivore Restaurant	4	011 950 6000		www.recreationafrica.co.za
9. Cedar Country Lodge	3	011 954 4049		www.cedarlodge.co.za
10. Cradle Lodge	4	011 956 4049	082 575 1786	www.cradlelodge.co.za
11. Croco Lodge Featherbrooke	3	011 662 1913	083 255 4520	www.crocolodge.co.za
12. Die Ou Pastorie Guest House & Restaurant	3	012 207 1027	083 228 0059	
13. Eagles Eyrie	5	083 616 6075	083 616 6075	www.eagleseyrie.co.za
14. Ekudeni Resorts	3	011 021 2186	082 449 3669	www.ekudeni.co.za
15. Forum Homini Boutique Hotel	5	011 668 7000	073 407 4869	www.forumhomini.co.za
16. Glenburn Lodge	3	011 668 1600	082 552 0895	www.glenburn.co.za
17. Hakunamatata	4	011 794 2630	084 701 4803	www.hakunamatata.co.za
18. Hayward's Luxury Safari Camps	5	011 442 5640		www.haywardsafaris.com
19. Heia Safari Lodge	3	011 919 5000	083 448 4993	www.heia-safari.co.za
20. Holmleigh Lodge	2	012 207 1271	083 267 8015	holmleighlodge.co.za
21. Kilulu Lodge	4	071 608 9380	072 278 9258	www.kilululodge.co.za
22. Kloofzicht Lodge	5	011 317 0600	072 516 7125	www.kloofzicht.co.za
23. Koelenrust Estate	3	011 659 0774	082 442 8768	www.koelenrust.co.za
24. Kwa-Empengele Cottages & Lodges	4	012 205 1833	082 755 4536	www.wheretostay.co.za/ kwa-empengele
25. La Chaumiere Guest House	3	012 205 1007	086 624 9642	www.lachaumiere.co.za
26. Leopard Lodge	4	011 701 3587	082 823 1187	
27. Lethabo Estate	4	082 654 1690	082 654 1690	www.lethaboestate.com
28. Linquenda Landgoed	3	073 563 5055	073 563 5055	www.linquendalandgoed.co.za
29. Malina Country Lodge & Fishing Estate	5	011 957 0229		www.malina.co.za
30. Maropeng Centre	4	014 577 9000	082 451 2934	www.maropeng.co.za
31. Maropeng Hotel	4	014 577 9100		www.maropeng.co.za
32. Misty Hills Country Hotel	3	011 950 6000		www.recreationafrica.co.za
33. Monchique Guest House	4	082 551 0851	082 551 0851	www.monchique.co.za
34. Ngomo Safari Lodge	4	011 662 4900	082 947 4071	www.ngomolodge.co.za
34. Ngomo VIP camp	4	011 662 4900	083 300 2906	www.ngomolodge.co.za
35. Oakfield Farm	4	010 590 2041	082 606 6000	www.oakfield.co.za
36. Protea Hotel Lesedi Cultural Village	3	012 205 1394	082 903 6996	www.lesedi.com
37. Random Harvest Cottages	3	011 957 2758	082 553 0598	www.random-harvest-nursery.co.za
38. Rhino Lodge	3	011 701 2242	082 451 0869	www.rhinolodge.co.za
39. Rothbury Country Lodge	4	012 205 1110	084 813 2871	www.hartebeespoortdam.co.za /rothbury/index.htm
40. Shumba Valley Lodge	4	011 790 8000	082 925 4623	www.shumbavalley.co.za
41. Squires on the Dam / Lake Motel	4	012 2531001	083 258 6839	www.squiresonthedam.co.za
42. Sterkfontein Caves	3	011 668 3200		
43. Sterkfontein Heritage Lodge	3	011 956 6307		www.sterkfonteinlodge.co.za
44. Sulla Via Conference Centre	3	011 954 5102	082 477 4308	www.sullavia.co.za
45. The Guest Suite at Take Time	4	011 794 2840	082 899 5087	www.taketime.co.za
46. The Moon & Sixpence	4	011 659 0429	082 887 0688	www.moonandsixpence.co.za
47. Toadbury Hall Country House	5	079 512 0554	079 512 0554	www.toadbury.co.za
48. Valverde Country Hotel	3	011 659 0050	072 587 0361	www.valverde.co.za
49. Villa Paradiso Country Estate	4	012 253 1847	082 828 6647	www.villaparadiso.co.za